My Rotary Journey

To Victoria

My Rotary Journey

A Memoir of a Rotary International Ambassador

Woodrow "Wooj" Byun
변우진(卞宇鎭)

Two Harbors Press,
Minneapolis

Two Harbors Press
322 First Avenue N, 5th floor
Minneapolis, MN 55401
612.455.2293
www.TwoHarborsPress.com

While all the incidents described in this book are true, certain events
have been compressed, consolidated, or reordered to ensure continuity.
All dialogue is as close an approximation as possible to the conversations
that took place, to the best of the author's recollection.

ISBN-13: 978-1-62652-873-4
LCCN: 2014908401

Distributed by Itasca Books

Cover Design by Kristeen Wegner and Biz Cook
Typeset by Mary Kristin Ross

Printed in the United States of America

Contents

Foreword vii

America and Me 1

    Out of Asia 3

    Welcome to America! 11

    Law School 19

    Half-Iowan Girl Pissed Off My Parents 29

    How to Help 120 Korean Grandparents Pass the US

    Citizenship Interview 35

    "Hold Your Wife's Legs!" 43

    Twenty Thousand Adoptees from Korea 49

    99.99999997 Percent Match 55

    Hanbok Bank 63

    Hee Ah Lee: The Four-Fingered Pianist 69

    Mr. Rocky, Peter Jennings, and a Liquor License 75

    China Boy Singing an Irish Song! 81

    Money and Happiness 87

    Courtroom Diversity: How Not to Look Like a Felon 97

Irish + Nepalese = Success.. 103

Russian Astronaut's Pencil 109

Life after Fifty.. 117

Rotary and Me 121

Rotary Is Enough Guarantee to Trust You 123

Why Do People Join Rotary?... 131

Children and Rotary 139

Purchasing a House, Rotary Style 143

Polio Eradication... 151

A Rotarian Taught Me How to Pray 157

Moses Miracle 163

Chinese President's Iowa Rotary Visit 167

We Shall Meet Again.. 171

Lessons I Learned from Rotarians 177

Who Needs a Speaker?.. 181

Feed My Starving Children 185

Do Good Anyway 191

Epilogue.. 197

Foreword

It is always my great pleasure to encounter a product of Rotary in an unexpected place. In May 2011, I met Mr. Byun in New Orleans at the Rotary International annual convention. Mr. Byun somehow found our group, probably drawn by our strong southeastern accent of the Korean language. It didn't take much time for me to discover that he was the recipient of our Rotary district's International Ambassadorial Scholarship more than twenty years ago. Some of the Rotarians, who came with me from Busan, Korea, to participate in this convention, recognized Mr. Byun. We were all so happily surprised to see him. To celebrate our reunion, we invited him out to dinner. Mr. Byun told us how the scholarship we gave him twenty years ago transformed his life and how instrumental it was in helping him realize his dream of becoming a global citizen.

We were so pleased to hear how he had developed a keen interest in Rotary since receiving the scholarship. He also told me that he would become the president of Edina Rotary Club, the second largest Rotary club in District 5950. I was particularly impressed by his willingness to serve, which, according to him, was his way to pay back to Rotary. We were touched by his message because, when we gave him the scholarship, we never expected him to pay back in any way. Since our brief reunion in New Orleans, he and I exchanged a few emails. Recently he told me that he just finished his term as president of the Rotary Club of Edina, and I congratulated him for this remarkable achievement.

I am proud of Mr. Byun for becoming a Rotarian, among other accomplishments in his life. As I recall, not many former recipients of Rotary's International Ambassadorial Scholarship actually became Rotarians. I am also proud of him for his willingness to serve as the president of the best Rotary Club in Minnesota. (He tells me that his club is best in the world, not just in Minnesota! I believe him.) He must have worked hard to overcome all of the cultural differences and difficulties to become an international lawyer and also a fine Rotarian in the United States. My fellow Rotarians in Busan, Korea, all agreed that the small seed we planted in a boy more than two decades ago has blossomed beautifully.

I would like to thank Mr. Byun for sharing his hard-earned Rotary story with us. I have no doubt that this memoir will encourage many young people who have thought about joining Rotary or helping people in need. I believe that Rotarians around the world will see this memoir as a reason why we should continue to support young scholars who want to broaden their horizons by studying overseas. By the time the readers finish reading this memoir, they will realize that the author completed a full Rotary circle by remaining faithful to Rotary's spirit of "service above self" for the past two decades.

On behalf of all the Rotarians in Korea, I would like to thank everyone who participated in taking care of our boy, who started a small, yet global, step with a scholarship we gave him long ago and who still continues a most remarkable Rotary journey. Throughout this fascinating trek, Rotarians on both ends of the Pacific Ocean somehow helped him complete his Rotary circle by giving him the opportunity to serve others, and also to become a fine Rotary leader, as well. Which reminds me of another purpose this memoir should serve—a bridge of international friendship among people around the world!

Hong Joo Yoon, MD, PhD
Governor of District 3660 in 2010–11
Arch C. Klumph Society Member 2012

America and Me

All of our people all over the country—except the pure-blooded Indians—are immigrants or descendants of immigrants, including even those who came over here on the Mayflower.

—Franklin D. Roosevelt

Out of Asia

> In the sky, there is no distinction of east and west; people
> create distinctions out of their own minds and then believe
> them to be true.
>
> **—Buddha**

I was born in Korea in 1962 to an elementary school teacher and
a homemaker. In 1988, after obtaining a BA degree in linguistics
at Seoul National University, and then obtaining a master's degree
in international law at Korea University in Seoul, I was looking
for a global opportunity to broaden my horizons. An internship
opportunity at the Hong Kong branch of an American corporate
law firm, called Coudert Brothers, looked attractive. I had a brief
interview with the firm's associate, named Thae Khwarg, who said
I was hired because I made him laugh with my "exceptional" sense
of humor. After hearing that I was accepted at this law firm as an
intern, I applied for a passport and a visa from the consulate office
of Hong Kong in Seoul. At the age of twenty-five, I left Korea for
the first time.

The year 1988 was an exciting time for me in many respects.
It was the year when Korea hosted the Summer Olympic Games

for the first time in its history. It was my first time to have a job, and I was thrilled that I would be working with fascinating people from all over the world. When I arrived in Hong Kong, China and Britain were already discussing the transfer of Hong Kong back to China after being under British rule for almost ninety years. The two superpowers had agreed in 1897 that Britain would rule this franchised city for ninety-nine years and then return it to China in 1997, but people in Hong Kong had mixed feelings about this transfer. Wealthy Hong Kong citizens were already leaving for Canada or Australia in anticipation of the transfer, and Chinese bureaucrats coming from Beijing were replacing their British counterparts, who were occupying high-ranking government positions in Hong Kong. After living under the British government for more than ninety years, Hong Kong's citizens became too used to democracy, and they strongly resisted returning to China's socialist regime. I often felt sympathetic toward my colleagues. However, as I knew there was very little that I could do to change their future, I merely decided to focus on my work.

Back then, Hong Kong was a stepping-stone to China for many foreign companies, including Korean conglomerates. My job was to help these Korean corporate clients in connection with their investment and transnational disputes in China and other Southeast Asian countries. Coudert Brothers was one of the world's largest and oldest international law firms when I went to its Hong Kong branch in 1988. Sadly, this firm, with more than five hundred smart lawyers with impressive degrees and backgrounds, has since dissolved. It was my first (and probably the last) opportunity to meet and work with Americans, Brits, Australians, French, and Hong Kong Chinese under the same roof. Since my plan was to stay with the firm for just one or two years before going to a law school in the United States, I decided to have as many experiences and meet as many interesting people as possible.

My boss was a lawyer named David Halperin. He was once an assistant to Dr. Henry Kissinger, but he decided to practice law in Hong Kong instead of building a public servant's career in

Washington, D.C. David was a heck of a lawyer, and as soon as I met him, I knew he would have a long-lasting impact on my life. He was more than a boss to me. In a very short period of time, he became a combination of teacher, mentor, friend, soul mate, and parent. He was truly my role model, and he still remains one as I write this memoir.

David was always nice to every person in the firm, ranging from senior partners to mailroom clerks. As far as I can remember, he was the only lawyer in the office who regularly said hi to the employee we called the "tea lady," an old and often-ignored Chinese woman. When she smiled, she showed several golden teeth that sometimes scared me. I saw her working only when someone in our office needed a cup of tea, and we usually ignored her because she hardly spoke any English. David didn't know any Chinese, but it didn't matter. He always said "zhou-shan" ("good morning" in Cantonese) to her, and the tea lady responded in Chinese with a big smile on her face. David and the tea lady never understood each other, but their relationship was always good because they never misunderstood each other either. If I have been nice to my employees at any time, it is because I learned from David Halperin the importance of being sincere and kind to everyone in the workplace.

After spending one year in Hong Kong, I decided to apply to graduate schools in the United States. Personally, I was more interested in an MBA (business) program; however, my father put a lot of pressure on me to become a lawyer. Not knowing what to do, I applied to ten MBA programs and fifteen JD (law) programs. I tried to save money in Hong Kong, but it was not easy. I heard through the grapevine that the Rotary Club in my hometown of Busan, Korea, was looking for ambassadorial scholars. Desperately in need of funds, I submitted an application and flew to Korea for an interview. This was my first encounter with Rotary. Up until then, I merely thought Rotary was a group of wealthy executives who wanted to brag about their money and social status.

On my way to Korea from Hong Kong, I read about Rotary to prepare for the interview. The more I read about the organization, the more I discovered my view of it was either wrong or limited. Contrary to my stereotypical notion that it was just a group of wealthy businessmen, Rotary actually meant much more. Rotary International (also known as the Rotary Club) is an international service organization whose purpose is to bring together business and professional leaders in order to provide humanitarian services, encourage high ethical standards in all vocations, and help build goodwill and peace in the world. Its membership is open to all people, regardless of race, color, creed, religion, gender, or political preference. There are more than 34,000 clubs and 1.2 million members worldwide. The members of Rotary Clubs are known as Rotarians. Members usually meet weekly for breakfast, lunch, or dinner, which is a social event as well as an opportunity to organize programs on their service goals. Rotary's primary motto is "service above self."

When the Rotarians in Busan began to interview me, I realized these folks were very serious about world peace by sending ambassadorial scholars around the world. Partly humbled by this realization and partly because of the booklets I read on my way from Hong Kong to Korea, I did well in the interview. Out of more than thirty applicants, I was lucky enough to become one of the five finalists who eventually received a "Rotary Ambassadorial Scholarship," which covers all the recipient's expenses for the first academic year overseas. I still remember what Dr. Yoon, the district governor back then in Busan, said to me toward the end of the interview: "This scholarship will help you become a global citizen."

Of all the schools that accepted me, the University of Minnesota Law School looked most attractive to me, and I decided to go to there. My decision to apply there was due to another fortuitous connection at Coudert Brothers in Hong Kong, where I met Bill Mondale, who changed my life entirely. When I met Bill, he was a second-year student at the University of Minnesota Law School, and he had come to work at Coudert Brothers as a summer intern in 1989. I didn't know who he was at first, but toward the end of the summer, I realized he was the second son of Walter Mondale, former vice president of the United States.

I liked Bill. He and I both shared a keen interest in international issues, and we both liked foreign language studies. Even though his internship lasted only three months, we spent much of it together. He taught me a lot of things, including how to prepare for and survive three years of law school. I am embarrassed to admit that until I met Bill, I had never even heard of Minnesota. In any event, mainly because of Bill's encouragement, I decided to include the University of Minnesota among the other fourteen law schools to which I applied. Coincidentally, the University Minnesota was one of the only two law schools (the other being the University of Texas) that accepted me. I remember the University of Minnesota had the lowest application fee ($25.00), as opposed to Ivy League law schools' $150 to $200 per application. As I will describe later, it wasn't until I started law school that I learned what Bill did to help me. Also, a few years after I came to study at the University of Minnesota Law School, I discovered that Bill and Jennifer Park (my future wife) were working together at the same division of the attorney general's office in Saint Paul, Minnesota. Sometimes I am surprised at how small the world truly is.

After being accepted at the University of Minnesota Law School, I had a little more than six months to spend in Asia before heading to Minnesota. I was wondering what to do with this time when David Halperin offered me a job of managing one of the antique furniture galleries he owned in Hong Kong. I needed to save money for law school, so I accepted David's offer. During this period, I had a chance to read fascinating books on Asian antique furniture, written by scholars and collectors alike. One of the most interesting collectors was an American diplomat named Edward Wright, who collected and eventually donated more than six hundred pieces of antique Korean furniture and porcelain to the University of Minnesota. Back then, I had no idea I would eventually have a chance to see his collection.

The six months passed quickly. David wanted me to stay and

manage his gallery for another year. However, I knew it was time I left Hong Kong to broaden my horizons in a new world. Knowing that I decided to leave, David invited me to his house one day and gave me some of his shoes, shirts, ties, and coats. He told me that even though he had never been to Minnesota, he knew that winter there would not be the same as in Hong Kong and that I should bring enough warm clothes. I almost felt that he was my father in Hong Kong.

Just a few days before my departure, David asked me to come to his office. When I entered, there was a Chinese man, named Mr. Lau, who was holding a measuring tape around his neck. Without a word, Mr. Lau began to measure my body. David said, "You need a Brooks Brothers suit if you are interested in becoming an international lawyer or businessman." The next day, Mr. Lau delivered to my office a New York-style suit made with Hong Kong craftsmanship.

Another thing I should mention about David Halperin is that he gave me a book titled *Myself a Mandarin: Memoirs of a Special Magistrate*, written by Austin Coates in 1987. In it, this British lawyer, who became a magistrate in a country district in Hong Kong, found himself plunged into a Chinese world about which he knew nothing and had to learn everything like a baptism by fire. He introduced a dozen cases whereby he was totally puzzled and baffled because of cultural differences for which he was not prepared.

I found Coates's book fascinating. As the author dealt with cows, squatters, dragons, and quarrelling wives (which may be viewed as bigamy in America or England but not so in a remote village in China), the author managed to shed light on them as if the readers were sitting in the courtroom as the actual judges.

Perhaps David Halperin had a similar experience when he first came to Hong Kong, and he gave this book to me thinking that I would have a similar experience as I broadened my horizons in the United States.

In August 1990, I said goodbye to all my friends in Hong Kong. I was sad to leave my friends, who came from different parts of the world. Farewell, Hong Kong! Take care, David! My friends in Hong Kong, I will miss you guys dearly!

Before coming to Minnesota, I spent my last week in Korea, mainly to say goodbye to my family members and to thank the Rotarians in Busan who decided to give me the Ambassadorial Scholarship.

With my boss, David Halperin, in Hong Kong about Christmas 1989. I always felt he was like my father. I usually played the role of Santa during our firm's annual Christmas party.

(Photo Credit: Coudert Brothers)

Welcome to America!

The bosom of America is open to receive not only the opulent and respectable stranger, but the oppressed and persecuted of all nations and religions; whom we shall welcome to a participation of all our rights and privileges, if by decency and propriety of conduct they appear to merit the enjoyment.

—George Washington

When I was accepted at the University of Minnesota Law School in 1990, I realized my connection to America (and Minnesota) actually went back to 1967, when, as a five-year-old boy, I had a chance to see Mr. Hubert Humphrey, former vice president of the United States, who had come to visit my hometown in Korea. I was on the shoulders of my father, who was in the crowd to welcome this important politician from America. I don't know why Mr. Humphrey came all the way to Busan, but I remember his visit very vividly. Along with hundreds of other citizens of Busan, I was waving both Korean and American flags to welcome him as his sedan passed our humble neighborhood. My next encounter with a Minnesotan took place in 1989 in Hong Kong when I met a young law student from

11

Minnesota named Bill Mondale. He certainly changed my life by introducing me to a place called Minnesota and also his alma mater, University of Minnesota Law School.

On August 15, 1990, I took the long flight from Seoul, Korea, to Minnesota. The flight took more than half a day. I read, slept, ate, spoke with another passenger, and looked outside the window, and I found myself still above the Pacific Ocean. I discovered from reading the in-flight magazine that the international airport in Minnesota was named after Mr. Hubert Humphrey.

Then there was an announcement from the captain:

Ladies and gentlemen, this is your captain speaking. First of all, I apologize for bothering you. I know most of you are sleeping. We have a small emergency here. One of the flight attendants, Nancy, seems to have lost her engagement ring. The good news is she believes it is somewhere on this plane. The ring may not have much commercial value; still, it is very important to her. I know you are all tired, and I apologize again for bothering you with a rather minor problem like this. But, it is an emergency for her, and we would highly appreciate it if you could help her find her engagement ring. She tells me that the ring is made of gold and it has a small diamond on it. It has both her and her fiancé's names engraved on it, too. Let's help her. On behalf of all the crew, I would like to offer our sincere gratitude for your cooperation. Thank you very much.

While the captain was making this announcement, Nancy was pointing to her finger where the ring was clearly missing. Some of the passengers didn't understand English and were terribly concerned by the captain's announcement, partly because of the desperate look on Nancy's face. We began searching for the lost ring. It is possible that some thought there was a mouse running around or a time bomb ticking somewhere on the plane.

About half an hour later, from one corner in the back of the plane, an old grandmother shouted, "I found it. Here it is! Nancy, I found it!" We all cheered at this discovery. Those who slept through and didn't participate in this fire drill also woke up because of the commotion on this trans-Pacific flight. When the fuss subsided, there was another announcement. This time it came from Nancy:

> Ladies and gentlemen, this is Nancy speaking. I would like to thank you for saving my marriage. This ring means a lot to me. Since I found my ring, we will turn off all the lights, and you may go back to sleeping or reading or whatever you were doing. The captain just allowed me to say this to you. As a token of our appreciation, we will serve you ice cream. If you would like some, please keep your eyes open. Again, thank you very much for saving my marriage.

This was my first encounter with a bunch of Minnesotans. They were all tall, blond, and many were blue-eyed (because of their Scandinavian heritage). They seemed to have a strange sense of humor. They woke me up in the middle of the night, asked me to find a ring, allowed me to go back to sleep, and then offered an ice cream. After living in Minnesota almost twenty years, I sometimes feel I have become a Scandinavian myself, but back then, I thought to myself that they had a unique way of thinking that was totally different from mine. Would I offer someone an ice cream if I woke him up to do me a favor? I am not sure.

Once I arrived in Minnesota, I quickly discovered the majority of people here were Scandinavians or those who came from Northern Europe. Many people asked me where I came from, since I didn't look like someone from Sweden or Norway. More considerate or sophisticated people asked the same question in a slightly different way: "Where did you come from originally?" I used to say I came from Korea, but now I tell them that I may be a Scandinavian myself. If anyone shows more interest beyond my initial response, then I tell them how I met Mr. Humphrey when I was only five years old and how I met Bill Mondale in Hong Kong in 1989 and how these encounters changed my life.

After arriving in Minnesota, I realized I had about three weeks before school started. I stayed with a Korean-American roommate, named Andrew Y. Kim, who was a third-year law student. I received a lot of help from him. His apartment was located in a place called Loring Park, where I went to walk to see the lake every evening. It didn't take much time for me to discover that this is a lake where men (yes, men!) were allowed to kiss each other. I thought to myself: "Scandinavian Americans in Minnesota must be very liberal and progressive."

About one week after I arrived, my roommate and Bill Mondale took me out to a Mexican restaurant to welcome me to Minnesota. When we finished dinner and stepped outside, it suddenly began to rain. Andrew, looking up at the sky, said, "Shit!" As soon as I heard the word, I assumed it was an American slang word for "rain," and I developed a habit of shouting, "Shit!" every time it rained or snowed. People seemed to understand me.

One afternoon, while studying in the library, I overheard someone saying, "Bullshit!" and I immediately looked out the window to see whether there was a shower or thunderstorm. It was sunny, and I realized that "bullshit" had nothing to do with rain. Out of curiosity, I looked in a dictionary to get to the bottom of shit and bullshit. Almost an entire year had gone by before I learned what those words actually meant. Since that day of enlightenment, I became an expert on these words, and have avoided using them, particularly when it rained or snowed or when something fell from above.

I still remember my first impressions of the United States when I came here in 1990. Here are a few of them:

1. People are kind. From the airport to the department stores to the post office to the library, people were kind. Literally, everyone said things like "Hi" or "How can I help you?" or "Thank you" or "You are welcome."

2. Everything was much bigger than in Korea or Hong Kong—the lakes, roads, cars, the Scandinavian people I met, McDonald's hamburgers, soda cups, and trees.

3. Dogs didn't bark. I always thought in my early life that the role of dogs was to protect their owners and their property by barking and biting, if necessary, but most American dogs I bumped into were friendly, just like their owners, and didn't bark or bite. I concluded later that Americans like to own dogs because they are the best quiet and trustworthy friends.

4. There are lots of advertisements and commercials in every aspect of American life. Advertisements on TV, radio, newspapers, buses, taxi cabs, Tiger Woods's hat, bulletin boards, and electricity poles all seemed to inundate an already complicated American lifestyle. Virtually every famous person was somehow related to certain marketing or commercial activities.

5. Americans didn't fart. Since I came to the United States, I never heard anyone farting openly. I at one point made a premature conclusion that Americans digest their food better than people in Korea or Hong Kong, but I withdrew this conclusion after realizing that there were many medicines sold in America dealing with upset stomach and indigestion, which probably help prevent Americans from farting. Perhaps Americans fart at home early in the morning before leaving their house, or they postpone farting to weekends or something like that. To my surprise, I never heard anyone farting in the public since I came to America.

6. Money seemed to be available everywhere. As the song "American Dream" goes in the musical *Miss Saigon*, with 10 percent down, people in America could get anything they wanted because the remaining 90 percent is easily available from the bank. This easily available money seems to enable Americans to own things, such as houses, cars, boats, furniture, and jewelry. Even students can borrow money from the bank and go to colleges

and universities, unlike their Asian counterparts, who usually borrow money from their parents to continue to study.

7. Medical doctors took time to explain why I became sick, instead of just prescribing medicine, which was my experience when I was younger. I guess it may have to do with American patients' tendency to bring medical malpractice lawsuits against their doctors. Regardless of the reason, I have been impressed by American doctors' kind explanations every time I became sick.

8. Coins played an essential role in American life. Without coins, you cannot park your car, purchase M&M's chocolate candies from a vending machine, photocopy documents, or clean your dirty laundry. Americans need to carry coins to survive on a daily basis.

9. Americans like to display impressive messages—political, commercial, or personal—on their cars such as: "Student driving"; "Proud parent of Saint Thomas University student"; "Say No to War!"; "Just married"; "If you see this sign, you are driving too close to me."

10. It is always personal injury lawyers who advertise on the last page of the yellow pages, and they always have 1-800 toll-free numbers so that people can call them without having to shuffle the thick phone book or worry about the cost of the urgent phone calls to reach a lawyer.

11. American people never go outside without putting on some sort of perfume. At least for the first month or so, I suffered from a severe headache every time I was confined to a classroom or restaurant because of the perfume people wore. I later discovered that magazines had perfume samples tucked inside.

12. Most houses in America didn't have fences. When I lived in Korea, all the houses we lived in had seven-foot-tall fences for privacy and protection from burglars.

13. Nonprofit organizations are an essential ingredient of the American society. It was a pleasant discovery that most of the

hospitals, churches, and schools were nonprofit organizations where employees were as hard working as their for-profit counterparts.

14. Only judges and ordained pastors can perform wedding ceremonies in America, whereas professors and teachers usually perform wedding ceremonies in most Asian countries, such as Korea or Japan. My father, who retired as an elementary school principal in Korea, gladly performs wedding ceremonies for his former students, but my father-in-law, who retired as a professor in New York, never had the honor to do so.

15. A microwave oven is a must have in the American kitchen. Every household has at least one microwave, and there are plenty of books on quick and simple microwave recipes. When I wrote to my mother about a microwave oven, she was worried I may be exposed to radioactivity by using it too much. I told her it is perfectly safe, although I had no scientific evidence on my side to support my argument.

16. Americans achieve marvelous things while driving. There are hundreds of things Americans can do either as a driver or as a passenger: ordering McDonald's hamburgers and French fries, watching a movie, listening to music or audio books, calling a friend, or having a physical relationship with someone, too, as long as one can control the car!

17. Americans always tip serving people, such as housemaids, cab drivers, or waitresses at restaurants or hotels, but they don't tip postal workers or cops.

18. Recycling is an important part of life in America. For many Americans, recycling newspapers, cans, and bottles is as important as sending their children to school. If a couple divorces, it is called "spouse recycling" in certain parts of America.

19. Americans know how to form a line and move in an orderly way. Americans know how to deal with four-way stop signs while

driving. It was a new concept for me, and it took some time for me to get used to it.

20. In the obituary, the family usually requests that, in lieu of flowers, memorials be given to a designated charity or the dead person's alma mater, or sometimes a tree be planted in memory of the dead person. I grew up in a culture where we always paid condolence money to the bereaved family members so that they can pay the funeral expenses.

Law School

Mister Hart, here is a dime. Take it, call your mother, and tell
her there is serious doubt about you ever becoming a lawyer."
                                   —Professor Kingsfield, *The Paper Chase*

I don't think I can squeeze my three-year law school experience into
a couple of pages. Typical law school experiences can be found in
many movies and books, so I would like to avoid it. The following
episodes are still vivid in my memory, however. My classmates and
I would never experience anything like this again in our lifetimes.

                         *   *   *

About one month after I began law school, Dean Robert Stein said
he wanted to see me. After more than fifteen years of service, he
was one of the longest-serving deans in the United States. Everyone
said he was a legend. Nervously, I entered his office.

"Welcome, Wooj. Please sit down." Dean Stein kindly shook
my hand and patted me on the back. I quietly sat down on the sofa
across from his desk, not knowing what to say.

He continued, "So how is law school treating you? Do you have any
problems? If you do, please do not hesitate to come to see me at any time."

"Thank you, Dean Stein," I said. "Other than the amount of

reading I have to deal with every day, I am generally doing fine."

Leafing through some documents that looked like my personal file, Dean Stein said, "Wooj, are you related to the Mondales by any chance?" I widened my eyes. Of course, I knew Bill Mondale since I met him in Hong Kong, but I never regarded him as my blood-related brother. I didn't know what to say.

"Well, you don't have to answer my question. But I would like to tell you that we received a recommendation letter from Fritz (Walter) Mondale on your behalf. You see, we rarely get a vice president's recommendation letter, if you know what I mean."

All of a sudden, I realized how I was accepted at the University of Minnesota's law school—Bill must have taken an extra step to help me get into his alma mater by asking his father to write a letter of recommendation for me, even though his father had never met me. It was then that I made a determination to finish law school by any means, if for no other reason than to make my friend Bill and his father proud of me. I felt very flattered, and yet I also felt a certain pressure on my shoulders. As I left Dean Stein's office, I told him I would do my best to graduate and contribute to improving the relationship between Korea and the United States. To this date, I can't thank Bill enough.

I met Professor/Dean Dean Stein at U of MN Law School's 125th anniversary, about twenty-three years after I first met him.

*   *   *

Law school was not an easy place for me. I don't know how I survived it. Since I had never before attended any school in the United States, I had an extremely difficult time keeping up with the reading assignments the professors enjoyed giving us daily. It was a handicap for me to not have the same historical and cultural background as my fellow students. For example, during constitutional law class, concepts like racial discrimination and affirmative action were hard for me to understand. Being new to the United States, I had no idea what it would feel like to be in one of those situations. But somehow I passed all the courses I took at law school.

Most of the law school students didn't watch TV, but I watched TV a lot, partly because I wanted to understand American people and their culture. One night Jay Leno said, "Michael Jackson signed an agreement to freeze his body before he dies. He will wake up about fifty years later when future medical technology can treat his skin problem. How about this? Let's all hide when he wakes up!" Sometimes I wished my professors at law school were as interesting as Jay Leno, who never failed to make me laugh.

About two months after starting law school, something most bizarre happened to me, which was very similar to what Jay Leno said on his show. When I went to class one morning, I could not find a single soul! I immediately thought one of the following scenarios had happened:

1. It was the university's or law school's Establishment Day, and everyone was celebrating the day at home (my experience in Korea was that I always stayed home for my school's celebrated Establishment Day, so this concept was nothing new for me); or

2. A war broke out and everyone stayed home to wait for further instruction; or

3. Everyone agreed to play a practical joke on me by deciding not to show up on that particular morning.

Because I was the only student at the law school who had never gone to any other school in the United States, I somehow thought my classmates were playing a practical joke on a massive scale. That particular morning, I went to Professor David Weissbrodt's tort class in room number 55, which was supposed to start at 8:00 a.m., sharp. But, nobody was there. Out of desperation, I went to room 45, 35, and 25 to see whether there had been a sudden change of rooms, but nobody was in those rooms, either. I went upstairs to see whether Tricia, the receptionist, was there. She was not there. Most confused, I decided to go home. Back then, we didn't have cell phones, and it never occurred to me that I should call my classmates to find out what was going on.

As I was leaving the law school building, however, I saw some students coming to school. When I recognized some familiar faces, I felt relieved. I asked them, "Do you know what's happening? Is there any problem with the school? I didn't see a single soul. Is everything okay?"

Everyone laughed and looked at me as if to say, "Hey, Wooj, where is the fire?" From the calm expressions on my classmates' faces, I was relieved to learn there was no war, thankfully, but I was still looking for a good answer. Then one student told me, "Wooj, did you know this morning we gained one hour by ending daylight savings time?" Without realizing that the previous night was the end of daylight savings time, I came to school exactly one hour early.

*   *   *

From the very first day at law school, I always erased the blackboard before every class, even though I knew very well that nobody expected me to do it. I guess I did it because I was taught in Korea that students should be ready to learn from the teachers with a clean blackboard and clean notebook. Many of my American classmates thought that I was a strange guy, and some even thought that I was trying to curry favor from the professors by cleaning the blackboard. I told them that I was doing it because I came from a culture where teachers and parents were respected to the same degree. I did it for the entire first semester before I was finally caught by Professor J.J. Cound, who taught the civil procedure class, which nobody understood anyway.

He said to me, "I have been wondering . . . Mr. Byun, why do you clean the blackboard? It is not your job."

I said, "Yes, I know it is not my job. But somehow it became my habit to clean the blackboard since I was young. My father has been a teacher all his life in Korea, and he always told me that teachers should be respected to the same degree as the students' parents or a country's king."

"Respect for teachers sounds good to me. But you are a student in America. You don't have a contract with the school to clean the blackboard. Nobody is paying you for this job. You may stop cleaning the board. Thank you."

Professor Cound reminded me that I was a student, not a janitor. He gave me B-, which should serve as a piece of evidence to all my classmates that I didn't get any favor from him by cleaning the blackboard.

* * *

Of all the new things I found in America, I found stand-up comedy the most fascinating. Americans may not know it, but stand-up comedy is a uniquely American phenomenon. In fact, Billy Crystal brought his stand-up comedy routine to Russia one time, but he realized quickly that Russian audiences didn't find his jokes funny at all. I guess certain jokes are so culturally unique to the comedian and his audience that they cannot possibly be translated and expected to be understood or laughed at by other audiences who don't share the same cultural background.

At the end of my first semester of law school, I began to feel an urge to participate in class discussions. Those who participated in the heated argument and lively discussion at law school always looked cool. For some reason, though, I decided to improve my speaking skills by joining a comedy club in Minneapolis. I knew it was crazy, but I decided to give it a try anyway. I developed a comedy routine of my own, practiced very hard in front of a mirror in my small apartment, and went to a place called Acme Comedy Company in downtown Minneapolis to test my jokes with the audience.

When I told the manger why I wanted to become a comedian, he laughed so hard he almost choked. He said, "Young man, you made me laugh, which is a good sign. But I would focus on law school if I were you. Out of twenty thousand comedians in this country, less than 1 percent makes any meaningful income. This is a tough business to survive, let alone become successful, in. If I were you, I would become a lawyer instead of a comedian. But, since you made me laugh, I will let you perform for five minutes every Monday evening for the next four weeks. The moment the audience stops laughing, I fire you. Do you understand me? By the way, your pay is unlimited beer at our club, as long as you make people laugh." Because my younger brother (Woomin Byun) became a famous actor in Korea, I knew for sure that I also had certain amount of performing arts DNA in me, and thought to myself that I would not fail in this comedy stint. Back then I was crazy about lawyer-bashing jokes, and I tried some of them at the club. Let me remember a couple of them here:

Two lawyers go into a cafe and order two drinks. Then they produce sandwiches from their briefcases and start to eat. The waiter becomes quite concerned and marches over and tells them, "You cannot eat your own sandwiches in here." The lawyers look at each other, shrug their shoulders, and exchange sandwiches.

Four surgeons are taking a coffee break and are discussing their work. The first says, "I like accountants to operate on. You open them up and everything inside is numbered." The second says, "I like to operate on librarians. You open them up and everything inside is in alphabetical order." The third says, "I like electricians. You open them up and everything inside is color-coded." The fourth one says, "I like to operate on lawyers. They are heartless, spineless, gutless, and their heads and rear ends are interchangeable."

The manager always introduced me to the audience as one of a kind—the only Asian comedian in town who also happened to be a law school student—and the audience all seemed to like my lawyer-bashing jokes. The manager had nothing to lose by allowing me to come to perform at his comedy club because I don't drink beer anyway. Even though I enjoyed every moment of this new experience, after performing three times, I had to give up this moonlighting career because I had to prepare for my second semester final exams.

I was once a comedian at Minneapolis Acme Comedy. It was toward the end of 1990. My salary was unlimited beer, which I didn't drink anyway.

Somehow, Dean Robert Stein heard about my comedy stint and asked me to perform at a distinguished alumni gathering. When I stood in front of a roomful of fifty-ish successful and impressive lawyers, I felt it was a totally different group from Acme Comedy. I remember I made them laugh anyway by telling the following jokes:

At the rate lawyers' numbers grow in this country, by the year 2050, 100 percent of Americans will be lawyers.

As you all know, the University of Minnesota Law School
has a very weird grading system. A+ is 16, A is 15, A- is
14, B+ is 13, and it goes down all the way to C-, which
corresponds to 8. At the end of my first semester, I got
mostly C+s, which equaled to 10 on my grade card. When
I called my father in Korea and reported that I got 10 on
all subjects, my father said, "Wooj, I am so proud of you.
You got perfect score! We have to celebrate." Beyond that
point I was destined to receive only C+s to make my father
happy.

In addition to the incident involving daylight savings time, I had to
learn many things the hard way. One time when I visited the home
of Professor Frickey, who taught us constitutional law, I heard him
calling his wife "honey," so I also called her "honey" throughout the
entire evening, assuming it was her name.

Another time when my classmate Andrea commented about my
jeans by saying they looked "cool," I honestly thought she meant I
looked cold. Those days feel so nostalgic to me now as I look back,
but somehow I survived each day, each week, each month, and each
semester, and, with good luck on my side, I managed to finish law
school and somehow pass the bar exam, as well.

I am embarrassed to admit that I did not pass the bar exam
the first time, but I somehow managed to pass it in February 1994.
To this day, I think I passed it largely because of my mother's
prayer. At every major turn in my life, my mother prayed for me.
As soon as I passed the bar exam, I shared the great news with
my five sets of parents, who were as happy as I was about this
major breakthrough. My parents included my biological parents in
Korea; David Halperin, who was my former boss in Hong Kong; Dr.
Yoon, governor of Rotary District in Busan, Korea; my parents-in-
law; and Bill and Lois Clynes (my godparents in Minnesota). The
boy from Korea who didn't know the concept of daylight savings
became an American lawyer, after finishing law school with the help
of the Rotary International Ambassadorial Scholarship.

At law school with Vice President Walter Mondale in 2013. The
University of Minnesota Law School was named after him in
2001. President Jimmy Carter also came to the dedication ceremony, to celebrate the life of Mr. Mondale. I discovered recently
that Mr. Mondale is a Korean War veteran, too. (Photo Credit:
Tim Rummelhoff)

Half-Iowan Girl Pissed
off my Parents

Marriage is nature's way of keeping us from fighting with
strangers.

—Alan King

When I saw my first Minnesota snow in 1990, I quickly discovered
this was not California's Santa Monica Beach or Florida's Key
West, which I saw in American movies when I was in Korea. After
I finished law school in 1993, I had a few opportunities to leave
Minnesota, but I didn't do it. Despite its cold weather, I somehow
became attached to the state and its beauty—the people were
kind, the environment was clean, and the education system was
outstanding.

I also discovered that Minnesota's contribution to the
development of several Asian countries has been extraordinary. For
example, Minnesota's Scandinavian residents have adopted more
than twenty thousand orphans from Korea, and the University
of Minnesota has taught more than four thousand scholars from
Korea for the past six decades. Minnesota has close to one hundred
thousand Korean War veterans. I often tell my friends in Korea that
I am surrounded by people who all have a big heart and giving spirit.

Encouraged by my small success as an amateur comedian at Acme Comedy Company and also at law school functions (in 1991, I was featured at the law school's newsletter for this "comedy" stint), I decided to test my jokes with the Asian lawyers in town. In February 1991, I went to a NAPABA Lunar New Year party. NAPABA stands for National Asian Pacific American Bar Association. It is a group of lawyers who share their Asian Pacific heritage. As I look back, it was a crazy attempt. Probably I was too ambitious to expect a bunch of Asian lawyers to laugh anyway. In spite of my best efforts, my stand-up routine at this event was a fiasco. No Asian lawyer found my jokes funny except, apparently, Jennifer Park, a practicing attorney in Minneapolis, who was amused and impressed by my endeavors. Years later, I discovered that she didn't understand my jokes at all; she was just impressed by the fact that I, a first-year law student straight from Korea, made so much effort to make people laugh. Regardless of how she was impressed, we began to date. Funny thing is that since Jennifer and I began to date, I gave up my stand-up comedy career entirely. Maybe I am still a comedian at heart, but Jennifer somehow turned me into a more serious person.

After a couple weeks of dating, Jennifer told me, "Wooj, I have to go to Duluth for two days for a court hearing. Why don't you give me a ring when I come back, say, on Thursday morning?"

There were many things I didn't understand about Americans, but this one caused my head to spin. I vaguely knew that American girls were quick, practical, and daring, but I didn't know they would be this fast. I immediately began to worry about my bank account balance, not knowing how much it would cost me to purchase a ring for this kind of occasion. I also worried that perhaps Rotary International didn't give me a scholarship to purchase a ring for a girl.

In law school, we sat in alphabetical order according to our last names. Usually I sat next to a girl named Amy Aug, who was a rather quiet and studious type. The next morning, before the class began, I told Amy the conversation Jennifer and I had, and I asked her opinion on what to do next. Amy laughed and said, "A ring in that context means a phone call." I felt so stupid and relieved at the same time.

Jennifer Park is half Korean and half Iowan. When I shared her ethnic background with my parents in Korea by telling them that she was only half Korean, my parents were half pissed off, thinking that she would understand and appreciate our cultural background only up to 50 percent. I was faced with double bummer. Jennifer's parents were also against our relationship for the same reason—they thought that I would never understand or appreciate the culture of Iowa. I admit I never made any genuine efforts to understand the people of Iowa. Seriously, Jennifer's parents were opposed to our relationship all the more because they thought I might force her to live in Korea, which might hurt her career, if nothing else. They somehow thought that an American man (preferably a Scandinavian one from Iowa) might make a better or more suitable husband for her.

Jennifer and I decided that we would get married sometime after I graduated from law school. As I am the oldest son, it was very important culturally to have the wedding in Korea. However, my father was against this idea. Being a Confucius scholar, and always regarding saving one's face to be more important than saving one's life, he thought it would help him save his face if we married in Minnesota as opposed to Korea, where a half-Korean bride would bring only half the honor to the family. So, just six weeks before my law school graduation, my parents informed me that we should have the wedding ceremony in Minnesota right after graduation because they were coming to the States anyway for my graduation ceremony. To make our parents happy and save their family honor, we set our wedding for May 22, 1993, in Minnesota, just twelve days after my graduation from law school.

Jennifer's parents lived in Buffalo, New York, and mine lived in Korea, so we had no relatives in Minnesota and had to plan the entire wedding ceremony and reception ourselves. It took every spare moment of the remaining six weeks to arrange everything, and we knew there were many items still missing, but we decided to go ahead anyway. Were it not for help from some people—such as Dr. and Mrs. Byung Moon Kim or Professor J. Y. Lee—I don't think our wedding would have been possible.

To save money, we decided to design and print our own invitations, instead of using a professional service. However, we thought we could make them look a bit more impressive by bringing the final version to Kinko's (a photocopy store). We parked in a ten-minute parking space, thinking that we would just quickly drop off the invitations, but then we ended up spending nearly an hour discussing the details, such as the color of the paper and fonts of the letters. When we came out to the parking lot, we discovered that our car had been towed! We then had to run to the nearest ATM to get cash for a cab to take to the towing lot, where we had to pay $140 to get our car back. Every penny we had saved by making our own wedding invitations went to the towing company! Jennifer still blames me for being too cheap to make the invitations the proper way, and I still blame her for not warning me about the strict towing laws in Minnesota. But somehow we got married and still live happily with each other.

When my parents came to Minnesota for our wedding, my father was most eager to meet Jennifer's boss, Skip Humphrey, the attorney general of Minnesota, because his father, Hubert Humphrey, was well known in Korea. Two days before our wedding, we visited Mr. Humphrey at his office. I told him about his father's visit to Busan in 1967 when his sedan passed our humble house, and then all of a sudden he beamed and said that he was with his father in the same sedan. Back then, he was a high school student, and he asked his father to allow him to go to see Korea, too. Mr. Humphrey told me that he heard about me from one of his associates, Bill Mondale. With that, we realized how small the world really was. At the end of our meeting, Mr. Humphrey joked by saying, "Wooj, I give you my permission to marry Jennifer, but please don't bring her to Korea yet. She is doing a fine job at the Minnesota Attorney General's Office, and I would like to keep her here as long as possible."

We invited about 150 people to our wedding, but the actual number of meals served surpassed 170 because about 20 Korean students just showed up without any invitation. They heard about our wedding through the grapevine and decided to celebrate the occasion by just showing up anyway. I didn't mind their presence because they came for the purpose of celebrating our wedding with us. Some of the guests were very special to us. In addition to Skip Humphrey, there was Robert Stein, dean of the University of Minnesota Law School, who has always been kind to me. Many of my dear friends from Hong Kong, who were now in the United States, also came. Bill Mondale, who introduced me to Minnesota, came as well. After the ceremony, Bill said to me, "I hope you don't hate me for bringing you to this bitter, cold state, but I am so happy that you found a girl with a warm heart."

Throughout my parents' entire visit, only our wedding day was rainy, but every guest showed up, and we all had a lot of fun. Jennifer and I were exhausted from planning the event. When the whole ceremony was over, we realized that something essential was missing in our wedding—our honeymoon! As we were totally lost in the planning of our own wedding ceremony, we somehow forgot to plan our honeymoon. Now those days all seem nostalgic and romantic to me, even though we made lots of mistakes. These days we joke to each other by saying that if we ever get married again (hopefully to each other), we will do a much better job!

As our parents predicted, we had many cultural differences. For example, I never grew up saying expressions such as, "Thank you" or "You are welcome" every time someone did something kind. During the first year of our marriage, Jennifer kept saying, "You are welcome" every time she served me water. I didn't get the signal until much later that she was expecting me to say, "Thank you." I guess she was trying to teach me good manners.

So one night we sat down and had a lengthy discussion on this topic. I told her, "Look, in our marriage perhaps fifty years from now, if we spare those expressions, then we save tons of energy. We are husband and wife now. Why bother to thank each other? Why bother to say, 'Thank you' and 'You are welcome' to each other thousands of times? After all, isn't it only natural for a wife to serve water to her husband when he is thirsty?"

Jennifer said, "Wooj, I don't want to have a double standard. I say 'Thank you' and 'You're welcome' to hundreds of other people. Are you telling me that I shouldn't show the same respect to my own husband? That's a double standard. And, when we have children, I want them to use those expressions all the time. In my opinion, it is barbaric not to thank people."

I said, "Wait a second. Are you telling me that my parents are barbaric because they don't thank each other? They lived like that for their entire lives. In fact, Korean couples lived like that for five thousand years, and they didn't divorce. How do you explain that?"

Not quite understanding this aspect of Korean culture, Jennifer said, "Okay, let's set a rule then. If we move to Korea, I will stop thanking you. In Korea, you don't have to say 'You're welcome' to me, either. But as long as we live in the United States, we should say 'Thank you' and 'You're welcome' until we die or divorce." Realizing that I could not possibly win this argument, I promised to live by that rule, but I admit it took a long time for me to become less barbaric by Jennifer's standard.

I always felt bad about not making a honeymoon trip with Jennifer immediately after our wedding ceremony, even though I think we had a perfectly good excuse—we had neither money nor time back then anyway. So in 2003, after ten years of marriage, partly to ease the weight of guilt from my shoulders and partly because I always wanted to visit these places anyway, we went to Paris and Rome. At the end of that trip, I declared to Jennifer and our two daughters that the trip to Europe was our belated honeymoon.

How to Help 120 Korean Grandparents Pass the US Citizenship Interview

The Constitution only gives people the right to pursue happiness. You have to catch it yourself.

—Benjamin Franklin

The Korean Service Center (KSC) in Minneapolis was established in 1990, mainly to help elderly Koreans living in the Twin Cities area. I served as its board member and advisor for a few years after its inception.

I believe it was a summer day in 1994 when Grace Lee, the outgoing executive director of Korean Service Center, asked me to visit her office. Sensing certain urgency in her voice, I hurried there. When I arrived, there were several people already in her office, including Reverend Jin Baik, Dr. T. H. Kim, and Ms. Hyon Kim, who just became a member of the board of regents at the University of Minnesota. Ms. Yoonju Park, who just succeeded Grace Lee, explained why we were summoned. According to her, the center's main customers—as many as 120 elderly Koreans, who have been living in Minnesota as green card holders—wanted to become US citizens, and they decided to help them in the process.

These 120 elderly Korean citizens, who already lived in

Minnesota for more than three or four decades, finally decided to embrace the United States as their new fatherland. Since they were exemplary citizens, and never had any criminal history whatsoever, their petition would be approved easily by the US Immigration and Naturalization Office. But there was a big hurdle in the process. These old Koreans had to have an interview and pass the oral test in English, which was a key element in becoming a naturalized citizen in the United States. None of the 120 old Koreans knew how to speak or write English fluently.

Some leaders in the Korean community suggested that we create a cram English course for these Korean grandparents. Many of us were not sure about this idea because these folks had very little time left before the interview.

Soon after the center decided to submit the petitions for 120 wannabe US citizens, Ms. Hyon Kim started negotiation with the immigration office in Bloomington about how to interview this large number of Korean elderly folks. The Korean Service Center invited me as a coach to help them prepare for the English interview. I prepared a handout of one hundred possible questions and answers for the naturalization interview. When I gave them the material, I quickly realized that these questions were way too hard for them to understand. Later, I discovered that these questions were hard for average American citizens, too. I could tell that some folks were too old to read the handout anyway. Some were holding the printed material close to their noses and still could not read it. Some just didn't understand English whatsoever. The situation was not very good.

As soon as I finished my first meeting with the applicants, I asked Grace Lee and Yoonju Park to reconsider this project, as it looked totally hopeless to me. But they said God will bless these folks, and things will turn out to be okay, eventually. I was not so sure.

Two days later, I received a phone call again from Grace. She told me that I somehow wreaked havoc on the Service Center residents. Apparently, many of the Koreans who received my handout began to have problems with their already weak health. Some suffered from insomnia; some threw up in the middle of night; and one even had a minor heart attack. Some seriously began to consider withdrawing the petition; some just cried; and some (still married) started fighting their spouses. And it was all because I told them to memorize the potential one hundred questions and answers for the US citizenship interview!

Realizing that some may die before becoming naturalized US citizens, I contacted the director of immigration's office and made a strong plea that we needed to narrow the questions down to less than twenty. When the director wanted to know why, I gave a detailed description of the kind of havoc I wreaked on the future US citizens' physical health. The director understood the seriousness of the situation and agreed to do so. After a few friendlier phone calls and email exchanges, we could somehow narrow down to only twenty questions and answers for the interview.

At the center's invitation, I went to meet the 120 elderly students again, who were still complaining about their headaches and ulcers because of my previous handout. I profusely apologized to them and handed out a revised printout of only twenty questions and answers. I told them to forget about the previous one hundred questions and asked them to memorize only twenty of them. Here are a few of them:

1. Who freed the slaves, causing the Civil War?
   Abraham Lincoln

2. Who was the first president of this country and is called the father of the country?
   George Washington

3. How many stripes are there on American flag?
   thirteen

4. How many years does the president serve after election?
   four

5. From what country did the United States gain its independence?
   England

6. What is the supreme law of the United States?
   the Constitution

7. Can you name three rights or freedoms guaranteed by the Bill of Rights?
   freedom of speech, freedom of press, freedom of religion.

8. Can you name three branches of our government?
   legislative, executive, and judicial

9. Who makes the laws in the United States?
   Congress

10. What are the first ten amendments to the Constitution called?
    the Bill of Rights

The Korean Service Center's four employees all helped in teaching the 120 elderly Korean petitioners to memorize these questions and answers. A few days before the interview, I conducted a simulated interview with a few randomly selected grandparents, just to see how this strategy worked. To my surprise, most of them passed.

But two people—Mr. Kim and Ms. Park—complained that they could not understand anything. For them, memorizing the twenty questions and answers was one of the biggest challenges in their lives. I know that they already invested a lot of money in the petition's filing fees, and they also spent many hours studying for the interview. I just had to come up with a solution.

I discussed the matter with my secretary at my office. She suggested a brilliant solution. She said, "It is simple. Don't try to teach a new trick to an old dog. Forget about the questions. You told me you and the immigrations director made the list together. That means that you both have the same list of questions and answers. Why don't you tell the Korean grandparents to remember only the answers?" I thought she was a genius. I gave her a big hug.

So the next day, I convened these two Korean grandparents again and asked them to memorize the answers first.

One day before the test, I conducted a simulated interview with Ms. Park and Mr. Kim to test my new strategy. From their viewpoint, the following happened:

1. Who @#$%?
   Abraham Lincoln

2. Who *&^%$#@?
   George Washington

3. How many $%#@!?
   thirteen

4. How many &^%$#@*?
   four

And so on. As I saw confidence on their faces, I kind of regretted the foolhardiness of my original strategy of trying to cram my original one hundred questions and answers into the brain of 120 elderly grandparents. Now, for Mr. Kim and Ms. Park, the strategy couldn't be any simpler: The first question's answer was Abraham Lincoln. The second question's answer was George Washington and so on.

The day dawned. When I went to the Korean Service Center, 120 most confident examinees, center employees, and all the volunteers from the Korean community were ready to greet the examiners from the Immigration Office, which included the director and six immigration officers. We had a quick ceremony, and the interview began in six separate rooms.

I began to bite my nails outside the rooms. From rooms 1, 2, 3, 4, and 5, grandmothers came out and beamed, "I passed! We all passed! Thank you, God! Thank you, America! Thank you, Mr. Byun!" They were almost in tears. Then second examinees entered and exited in exactly the same ecstatic way. When I was feeling great and relieved, it came to my attention that an examinee from room 6 took extra time, and she didn't pass the test. I went to see who it was. It was Ms. Park. She was totally disappointed. She was scratching her head. Another examinee entered the room, and he also came out disappointed. It was Mr. Kim. I spoke to both of them.

"What happened?" I asked.

Still denying that she failed the citizenship interview, Ms. Park said to me, "I did exactly what you told me to do. I said Abraham Lincoln after the first question. I said George Washington after the second question, and so forth. But somehow I failed."

The response from Mr. Kim, who also had his interview at room 6, was very similar. They both puzzled me.

Lunchtime came. After lunch I had a chance to speak with the room 6 examiner. He told me that he was not supposed to be on duty that day—he happened to replace an examiner who had a family emergency that morning. That explained why some of the unlucky grandparents who were assigned to room 6 failed the citizenship interview. Instead of asking the questions in order, the room 6 examiner randomly asked the questions. So the following happened in room 6 that morning:

1. Who was the first president of this country?
   Abraham Lincoln

2. Who freed the slaves, causing the Civil War?
   George Washington

3. How many years does the president serve after election?
   thirteen

4. How many stripes are there on American flag?
   four

5. Who makes the laws in the United States?
   England

6. From which country did the United States gained independence?
   the Constitution

And so on. As soon I discovered this rather humorous discrepancy between the randomly asked questions and thoroughly prepared answers, I thought something needed to be done in room 6 in the afternoon. So I asked Reverend Baik to team up with me to provide an interpretation service in room 6. When we explained the questions in the Korean language, the examinees had no problem answering the questions. Those who failed in the morning in room 6 were given another chance in the afternoon. Mr. Kim passed to our excitement, but Ms. Park still failed.

At the end of the day, we discovered that 119 out of 120 passed the test. The Immigrations Office director felt sorry for the only grandmother who failed the test, but he promised to offer another interview for her within one month.

The Korean Service Center and all the volunteers wanted to have a big party, but the 119 who passed the naturalization test said they should wait until the last person passed the interview. One month later, the last grandmother, who already knew the answers by heart, went to the interview again, and as everybody expected, she passed the test with ease.

A big ceremony ensued. When the judge handed over the US citizenship certificates to the 120 Korean grandparents, many of these new US citizens were shedding tears of joy. All of them, holding both Korean and American flags, celebrated their becoming new citizens of their newly adopted country. The *Star Tribune*, the biggest newspaper in Minnesota, covered this historic event. I was proud of these folks, who memorized names like Abraham Lincoln and George Washington, despite the fact that they never had any chance to attend any school in the United States to learn about them. As I looked around, many volunteers, including the Korean Service Center employees, Reverend Baik, Ms. Hyon Kim, and Dr. T. H Kim, were feeling the same degree of pride, as well.

After the ceremony, I approached Ms. Park, the 120th successful interviewee who trusted and faithfully followed my instruction throughout the entire process. I congratulated her on becoming a new citizen of the United States. Even though she was more than seventy years old, her smile was that of a teenager.

I myself became a US citizen in 2001.

"Hold Your Wife's Legs!"

> Coming together is a beginning. Keeping together is progress. Working together is success.
>
> —Henry Ford

"Until you have a child of your own, you will never understand your parents." My mother used to say this to us when we were young. I guess she was right. Raising my two daughters definitely helped me understand my parents.

If my daughters were born in Korea, they would have met their mother first. Because they were born in America, however, they met me first when they were born. You will see the reason below.

When our first daughter, Nina, was born, neither Jennifer nor I had any clue as to what was involved in childbirth. We went to a series of prenatal classes arranged by the hospital before delivery. Jennifer was taught to breathe like a marathon runner (twice out-breathing and twice in-breathing), which she should start as soon as the contraction begins and until, of course, the baby is born. My role was to make sure Jennifer breathed properly, like a coach to a marathon runner or a wingman to a pilot. The trainers also told us that we should prepare the most suitable music for the mother and bring it with us to the hospital when the MOMENT came. We—the fathers—also learned how to give mental support to our wives, but I am ashamed to admit I quickly forgot about most of the instructions the next day.

As soon as we came home from one of the prenatal classes, we designated a bag for the delivery day and packed it with essential items Jennifer might need on the day of delivery. It became quite bulky with items, such as a cassette player, two cassette tapes that contained Jennifer's favorite music, a novel, a note pad, two pens, hand lotion, and moisturized tissues. With this bag ready, there was very little to do on my part, other than occasionally help Jennifer with the dishes, carry heavy grocery bags, and so on. We placed the bag near the entrance area of the house so we could snatch it at any time.

I don't know why babies choose the weirdest time to come out, but in our particular case, Jennifer went into labor before dawn. Half asleep, I snatched the bag, and we drove to the hospital as fast as we could, with Jennifer screaming next to me all the way. Fortunately, nobody stopped me on the road, and I didn't get a speeding ticket.

When we arrived at the hospital, the triage was set already. Contrary to my expectation, however, Jennifer's cervix was not dilated enough, and the baby was not quite ready to come out. Jennifer screamed, "Wooj, can you play my Kenny G tape, please? Hurry!" So I took out the cassette player, which had her favorite Kenny G songs in it already. But as luck would have it, there was no music. After six months of no use, all the batteries in the cassette player were completely worn out. Maybe the radio was on, who knows? Feeling a bit sweaty, I asked the nurse whether there were six extra D-sized batteries in the room. The nurse stopped what she was doing and looked pathetically at me as if to say, "Are you out of your mind? Is this the best time to talk about D-sized batteries?" She simply said no. Jennifer grabbed my arm and yelled, "No music? How can you do this to me? No music? Give me my music, NOW! I need it NOW!" She was desperately grasping the bed sheet, and I just stood there with a mixture of embarrassment, stupidity, helplessness, and guilt. I felt it truly ironic that, under the circumstances, I was sweating more than she was. I thought of humming the songs if Jennifer truly wanted them, but decided not to, knowing that it would only irritate her even more. I just could not do anything.

I was about to go to a drug store to get six D batteries, but the nurses told me not to leave the room. As a matter of fact, one nurse said, "Mr. Byun, we want you to stay here in this room, and we want you to comfort Jennifer by holding her hands. But eventually we want you to hold her legs when she starts to deliver your baby. It could happen any minute, as you know."

I could not believe what the nurse just told me to do. HOLD HER LEGS? Are you kidding me? No way!

In many countries, including Korea, men are NOT allowed to see the moment of delivery. In five thousand years of history, Korea never allowed husbands to be in the same room with their wives at the moment of delivery. I felt comfortable enough handling things like coaching Jennifer's breathing or holding her hands or massaging her back, but holding her legs didn't seem culturally right or acceptable to me.

Wanting to be useful, I mustered some courage and took Jennifer's hands. And I told her, "Remember, Jennifer, we learned how to breathe—like a marathon runner. Follow me, Jennifer. He-he-ha-ha, he-he-ha-ha." At this suggestion, Jennifer looked at me seriously for a while and said, "Wooj, are you kidding me now? Breathe like a marathon runner? Just shut up! I will breathe my own way. You mind your own breathing. Just go away!" I felt guilty, humiliated, sweaty, and embarrassed again.

After many hours of contributing absolutely nothing to the situation, I felt hungry. I realized that I skipped both breakfast and lunch. So I excused myself by saying I needed to go to the bathroom. In the hallway, I bumped into another father whose wife was also in the process of delivering. Feeling that we were in the same shoes, we gladly said hi to each other. He was holding a camcorder. While chewing gum in a most relaxed way, he was replacing the batteries in the camcorder. I could tell that he was a well-prepared father and husband, unlike me, who even failed to mobilize a simple primitive cassette player. He also had a plastic bag, which had a lot of fruits, such as bananas, apples, and oranges, in it. Realizing that I was looking at his food, he said, "You must be hungry. I understand. Help yourself. Go ahead. I knew I would be hungry, so I packed these fruits last night. I think we should reserve our energy for the big moment, if you know what I mean."

I thought he was a nice guy, as well as a prepared one. I said, "Thank you!" Without a moment's hesitation, I took a banana from his plastic bag, admiring his preparedness and calmness under the circumstances.

As I finished two bananas from his bag, I suddenly became curious and asked him why he was holding a camcorder in a moment like this. He said, "Oh, this? My wife and I are so happy about our first child, who happens to be a boy, so we decided to record the moment of his birth. We had to save money to buy this camcorder. In fact, I call this my baby, too. So today, I have two babies. This will be my first time to use it. I am so excited! Wish me good luck!"

I thought to myself that even though his efforts were grand, and their first homemade film would be a valuable record of the couple's new life, I was a bit afraid that it would be an X-rated movie for sure. I also thought that, if he was interested in filming his son's life from the beginning, he should have purchased the camcorder nine months earlier, to start the movie from the moment of conception instead of from the moment of delivery.

As soon as I finished the bananas and he finished loading his camcorder batteries, we wished good luck to each other and entered our wives' bloody rooms again—he was holding a camcorder in his hand, loaded with new batteries, and I held banana peels in mine.

Jennifer's labor became intense, and again I was told to hold her legs. I tossed the banana peels in the garbage can and stood in front of Jennifer. I knew it was against my cultural upbringing, but because I knew Jennifer was mad at me for many things, including

Kenny G music, I didn't want to screw up again. So I decided to hold Jennifer's legs and added my voice to the doctor's and nurses'. "Push, Jennifer. We are almost there. Push!"

After twelve hours of labor, which was eleven hours longer than I expected, our first baby, Nina, was born. In my memory of other babies, all newly born babies had beautiful pink faces. But when I saw my daughter, I could not help thinking she looked like a Smurf. Instead of pretty pink or ivory, her face color was totally green! It was then that I knew the true reason why fathers in Korea were not allowed to witness the moment of childbirth. About one hour later, Nina's face color changed from green to healthy pink, much to my relief.

I called my parents and siblings in Korea to share my experience in the hospital. When I explained that I had to hold Jennifer's legs, among other things, everyone was surprised. But my mother's reaction was a bit different. She said, "That's a wonderful idea. After all, you men should realize how hard and painful it is for a mother to deliver a baby. I wish your father had that same experience when you and your siblings were born. You see, it is very easy to plant the seed, but it is very difficult to protect and cultivate that seed for another nine months. Son, I am sure it was a valuable experience for you to be with Jennifer at the moment of delivery. Next time, son, do it again without being told to by the doctor or the nurses. I am glad you had the 'American' experience. Good job. I am proud of you!"

When our second daughter, Maria, was born about three years later, I had much less cultural resistance to being in the delivery room and also to holding Jennifer's legs. This time the cassette player (actually it evolved to CD player) worked just fine, and I wasn't surprised at our baby's green Smurf face at all. As a matter of fact, while witnessing our second daughter's birth, I somehow felt that it made sense for the father to participate in the process of delivery by playing a small, yet meaningful, role.

I am my father's eldest son. My father is also the eldest son to his father. According to age-old Korean tradition, it is my duty to produce a son, so that our family name continues. After our second daughter was born, my father's reaction was very simple: "When are you going to have another child?" Every time he said this, I sensed he was waiting for news of a grandson, so I usually said, "Very soon!"

But after Jennifer and I both turned forty, we pretty much gave up the idea of having another child. As a full-time working mother over the age of forty, Jennifer said that having a third child would be too risky. Jennifer was thirty-seven when she was pregnant with Maria, and because of premature labor, she had to be hospitalized and remain on bed rest during the last trimester. I agreed with her that we should not have another child. Yet my father's inquiry continued for several years after our second daughter, Maria, was born. The last time I had this kind of conversation was after both Jennifer and I finally decided not to have any more children for sure. When my father asked me the same question again, I gave him the following answer: "Dad, I know my filial duty as the oldest son. I never forgot it. I am still diligently working on it. But Jennifer is NOT working on it. So it is not happening."

Since I became a citizen of the United States, where men and women are equal, I thought I don't have to produce a son to fulfill my filial duty as a good son to my own father. If there is any such need in the future, we can always adopt one, but it is very unlikely to happen. Jennifer and I are grateful we have two most beautiful and healthy children. When our two daughters have their own children in the future, I will tell their children that I am the first person their mothers met in this world, even though those encounters were against my cultural background. I am sure they will find it interesting.

Twenty Thousand Adoptees
from Korea

The only way to have a friend is to be one.

—Ralph Waldo Emerson

I heard that majority of Minnesotans are descendants of early settlers who happened to come from Scandinavia and northern Europe, although, recently, many immigrants came to Minnesota from Asia, Africa, and South America, as well. One unique aspect of Minnesota is that it also has the largest population of Korean adoptees, which exceeds twenty thousand. This is twice the number of Korean immigrants in Minnesota, which are fewer than ten thousand at most. There are many theories as to why there are so many Korean adoptees in Minnesota. I will relate a few of them.

Minnesota's first meaningful relationship with Korea happened toward the end of the Korean War (1950–1953). According to Don Montgomery, my dear neighbor and also the former secretary general of the Korean War Association of Minnesota, General MacArthur recruited young men from Minnesota in particular because he thought that they would know how to handle the cold weather of North Korea, which is similar to the weather in

Minnesota. Throughout the war, as many as one hundred thousand soldiers were sent from Minnesota to Korea, and these Minnesotan Korean War veterans brought home the sad stories of orphans of the Korean War. I heard many of these soldiers adopted orphans from Korea, and many other Minnesotans followed suit. Second, there is a wonderful adoption agency, called the Children's Home Society, in Saint Paul, Minnesota, with more than five hundred dedicated social workers, who have been instrumental in locating and bringing orphans from Korea to Minnesota. Third, Minnesota's Scandinavians (who are mostly Christians) like to adopt children. Interestingly, more than 90 percent of Korean adoptees go to colleges or universities after high school. I believe this is just one shining example of how wonderful and dedicated the Minnesotan adoptive parents are!

I heard from several people that, apparently, it was very difficult to be an adoptive family in the seventies and eighties, when there was little networking opportunity among the parents. But, gradually, the parents formed a network by publishing newsletters and getting together regularly and on major holidays. Every time the adopted families got together, the adopted Korean children were happy to see each other because, for the first time, they met others who looked exactly like themselves.

As the adopted children began to go to school, some parents thought it would be a good idea for the children to learn about Korean culture, language, and history on a regular basis. Fortunately, the University of Minnesota provided plenty of resources, including 350 graduate students from Korea at any given time, who could teach what the adoptive families wanted to learn. About 1978, Korean Culture Camp was launched in Minneapolis, Minnesota. When the camp opened, all of a sudden inquiries came from families in European countries, such as Sweden, the Netherlands, France, and Belgium. Apparently, there were at least fifty thousand Korean children adopted in those European countries, as well. However, there were no cultural camps available there. So this small camp in Minnesota became an international sensation soon after it first opened.

Today, the Korean Culture Camp (KCC) is one of the biggest and most successful among thirty or more similar camps around the United States. It celebrated its thirtieth anniversary in 2007. Because my two daughters were frequent participants of this camp, and I worked as a teacher there one year, I thought it would be meaningful if I somehow informed people in Korea about this international phenomenon called the Korean Culture Camp.

After thinking of many different ways to do this, I concluded TV would be the most effective medium. I sent numerous emails and made dozens of phone calls until I finally received a response from an international correspondent working for Korean Broadcasting System (KBS) in its Washington, D.C., office. KBS in Korea is equivalent to ABC or CBS in the United States, in terms of its audience size and impact. When I explained the history and importance of the Korean Culture Camp, Mr. Min, a reporter for KBS, agreed to come and cover the story. Before coming here, he collected a lot of information about Minnesota, the twenty thousand adoptees from Korea, and the Korean Culture Camp via the Internet.

The night before Mr. Min's crew was to arrive in Minnesota, there was a rumor that Cuba's Castro collapsed and might die soon. I did not see any connection between Castro and the Korean Culture Camp; however, as far as the Washington-based KBS TV crew was concerned, there was a priority conflict. The crew decided to cut short their trip to Minnesota from their originally planned five days to only two days, and, instead, they decided to go to Cuba immediately after Minnesota to cover Castro's deteriorating health. After all, Koreans in Korea would be more interested in Castro's demise than the Korean Culture Camp for adoptees in Minnesota. I understood the dilemma of this TV crew.

We now had only two days, so we decided to quicken and tighten up our schedule. As soon as the TV crew arrived in Minnesota, we (Mr. Min, the reporter; Mr. Lee, the camera operator; and I) rushed directly to the camp and began interviewing the campers, teachers, and volunteers. In order to save time, we had lunch with the campers and didn't leave the campsite until late at night.

Mr. Min was surprised to find the following facts:

1. All the Korean food, including Kimchi (Korean pickled cabbage) and Bulgogi (Korean barbecued beef), was cooked for the campers by volunteering parents in Minnesota. The food was nearly authentic in terms of taste, color, and flavor, even though it was made by parents of Scandinavian heritage.

2. The camp was nonprofit, but it was profitable every year, and the profit (roughly three thousand dollars every year) had been sent to Korean orphanages for the past thirty years.

3. Every year the number of campers ranged from about 300 to 350. The number of volunteering parents ranged from about 300 to 350.

4. The only paid people were teachers, who were typically Korean graduate students at the University of Minnesota. They were paid about fifty dollars per hour.

5. Most of the volunteering parents were working full-time, and they took a week's vacation from their employment to participate in the camp. Everyone was given an assignment, ranging from cook to guard to custodian to babysitter.

6. The campers ranged in age from four to twelve. More than 90 percent of these Korean adoptees eventually go to colleges and universities.

7. Every year, at least forty or more teen helpers volunteered, and they were all graduates of the camp. This teen internship became very competitive as the number of applicants surged to ten times more than the needed number.

8. Every year, at least 3 to 5 percent of the campers were not adopted Koreans. In other words, they did not come from Korea. They were typically relatives or siblings of the adopted children. Many of them were born in the United States to the parents who adopted children from Korea.

When our day's work was over, in the evening, we went to interview a family who adopted four children from Korea. With a short notice, Jim and Debbie Moe and their four children welcomed the Korean TV crew. The children ranged from seven to fourteen years of age. They were all wonderful students with excellent academic success and various other extracurricular achievements. I still remember what Debbie Moe said to us: "Our children made us Koreans. We may look Caucasian outside, but inside we are Koreans."

Summer in Minnesota is hot. The reporter, cameraman, and I constantly sweated like crazy because of the busy schedule. Mr. Lee was struggling with a heavy camera, tripod, and microphone, but there was no time to waste. We all cursed Cuba and Castro.

In the evening, we moved to another house to interview another adoptee and her husband. Approximately forty years ago, Melissa Wright was adopted by a family in Rochester, Minnesota, after her biological parents in Korea became terminally ill. She became a very successful lawyer and is happily married to her husband (of Italian heritage), who is also a lawyer. After having two children, Melissa wanted to learn more about her own heritage. She somehow found her biological brother in Korea and had been keeping in touch with him.

After spending two days in Minnesota, the KBS crew left for Cuba to cover Castro's death. I discovered later that Castro didn't die after all. Mr. Min called me to apologize for shortening the schedule in Minnesota. I told him it was not his fault; it was Castro's fault to become sick and not to die in the end.

KBS aired the documentary in October 2007. As many as twenty million people in Korea saw the program. Afterward, I shared the documentary with my friends in Minnesota, too, and they all told me that it was a good idea to document this extraordinary phenomenon known as "twenty thousand Korea adoptees in Minnesota." I was glad the documentary provided an opportunity for Koreans to realize that the adopted orphans have been well cared for by their wonderful parents in Minnesota, who made sacrificial efforts to give their kids the best life possible. I still believe Minnesotans and Koreans must have been related to each other some six hundred years ago. Otherwise, they wouldn't love each other this much.

99.99999997 Percent Match

The true meaning of life is to plant trees, under whose
shade you do not expect to sit.

—Nelson Henderson

My office's intern, Elizabeth, introduced her sister-in-law, a woman
from Iowa, to me. Her name is Anna Anderson. (I have changed her
name to protect her privacy.) Anna was adopted from Korea when
she was only seven months old.

Anna was too young when she was adopted to remember
anything now about her biological family. The only record she had
was her parents' names, which, unfortunately, were very common
like the American equivalent of John and Susan Smith. Since the
adoption, Anna grew up in a German immigrant family in a small
town. She shared with me photos from her Iowa family, which
showed that she had four brothers, who were all as tall and muscular
as Paul Bunyan, a legendary folklore hero in Minnesota. Anna was
twenty-eight years old and worked for a Fortune 500 company as a
software programmer.

"Why do you want to find your biological parents now?" I
asked.

"I cannot ask for more when it comes to my adoptive family's love and protection," Anna said. "I have had the most wonderful twenty-eight years with my parents and four brothers in Iowa. But since I got married last year, I could not help thinking about my biological parents. We will start a family of our own soon. When our first child is born, I would like to tell the child where I came from. My husband's ancestors came from Greece. My adoptive parents are German. Does it mean that I am a Greek or German, as opposed to Korean? I would like to tell our child that I am Korean. Without knowing who my biological parents are, I don't think I can call myself Korean."

I sensed that Anna had been thinking about this issue seriously and for a long time.

"Anna," I said, "our meeting is very timely. Korea Broadcasting System sent its TV crew to cover the thirtieth anniversary of the Korean Culture Camp in Minneapolis. Perhaps we can include you in the documentary so that your biological parents in Korea can see you on a national TV program. After all, millions of Korean viewers will watch this documentary—and who knows, your mother may be one of them."

"Really? That would be wonderful, but do you think they would cover my personal story?" asked Anna, still not believing what she heard from me.

I called Mr. Min, the TV reporter, to see whether he would have any time available to interview Anna. Mr. Min said he had time only between eleven p.m. and midnight, then he needed to go to bed for the next day's schedule. When I explained it to her, Anna said she would not mind waiting at the hotel lobby to meet the TV crew at eleven. She had been waiting more than twenty-eight years for this moment, and so she was certainly willing to sacrifice a few hours of her sleep.

At eleven p.m., Anna and the TV crew met in the lobby of the Holiday Inn hotel in Bloomington, Minnesota. Both Mr. Min (the reporter) and Mr. Lee (the cameraman) were deeply touched by Anna's efforts to find her biological parents in Korea. Here is how the TV interview went as I remember:

Mr. Min: Can you tell us who you are and who your parents are?

Anna: My American name is Anna Anderson. I am twenty-eight years old. I am a computer programmer. My Korean name is Min Joo Lee. My parents' names are Hyun Soo Lee and Young Hee Lee. I heard that these names are very common in Korea.

Min: Millions of viewers are watching this program. Tell us any information that may help find your parents in Korea.

Anna: When I was born, my parents were not married. They were too young to raise me. As a matter of fact, my father left my mother as soon as he discovered his girlfriend was pregnant. As a poor teenager, my mother was afraid to become a single mother. So she decided to send me overseas for international adoption. I was born on January 23, 1979. Unfortunately, I don't have any record as to my parents' birthdays or where they live today.

Min: May I ask how you were adopted into your current family?

Anna: I was with a temporary foster family in Seoul. Soon after that, an adoption agency in Korea and one in Minnesota jointly found a family in Iowa, who desired to adopt a girl from Korea. I was only seven months old when this happened.

Min: This program is broadcast all over Korea. Suppose your parents are watching this program. What would you like to say to them? Look at the camera and talk as if you are talking to your parents in Korea.

Anna, with tears in her eyes, choked briefly and said: "Mom, Dad, where are you? My name is Min Joo Lee. I am your daughter. Your names are Hyun Soo Lee and Young Hee Lee. You gave me my life twenty-eight years ago. I am doing very well now. I would like to meet with you so that I can tell my future children about their heritage. If you don't want to meet with me for any reason, I fully understand. But I sincerely hope that you decide to see me at least once. I have been waiting for this moment for the past twenty-eight years. Thank you."

Anna began to cry, and Mr. Min had to stop the interview. Even though quite poignant at times, I could tell that the interview went very well. Mr. Min said the interview of Anna was a good way to finish the documentary.

With the interview behind us, we went back to our normal lives. Anna went back to Iowa, and the TV crew went to back to Washington, D.C. Then about one month later, in August, we heard from Mr. Min that as many as five women in Korea came forward, all claiming they were the mother of Anna. Both Anna and I were wildly excited at this news. Knowing this was way too important an issue for both Anna and her mother, I suggested that we refer this matter to science. Anna agreed. So we cut about fifty strands of Anna's hair and sent them to Korea for DNA testing. A nail-biting month passed, and the test results finally came to us. To our shock and disappointment, none of them matched Anna's DNA. None of the five women's DNA came close enough to leave any room for future hope. When I broke this sad news, Anna was sobbing. After this most disappointing moment, we didn't communicate with each other for some time.

Over Christmas that year, Anna sent me a box of candies with a card. In the card, she wrote: "Dear Mr. Byun, I may not have expressed it often enough, but I truly appreciate what you have been doing for me. The mismatching DNA test was certainly disappointing, but I thought about it from a different angle. The five ladies all must have given away a baby like me to a family in the United States. As I want to become a mother myself, I began to feel their pain. I am sure my true mother is somewhere out there. It is just a matter of time before we find each other. I will never give up the hope of meeting her."

I am not a woman, and I will never know the depth of pain associated with giving birth to a child, or giving the child up for adoption for whatever reason. But when I saw the word "pain" in Anna's card, somehow I felt the pain. Then all of a sudden I felt the pain of all five women in Korea, and then the pain of all the mothers in the world, including my own mother. So I made a resolution: let's find Anna's mother no matter what.

When I looked at the lunar calendar, the year 2007 was the year of the boar, according to the Chinese Zodiac. The year 2006 was the year of the dog. I thought that boars would bring better luck than dogs. Sometime in January 2007, with a renewed determination, I met Anna again. I handed her a *hanbok* I kept in my office. Hanbok is a traditional Korean costume, and I thought that it could be a token of my commitment to finding her mother. Anna gave me a big hug.

Sometime in March 2007, I discovered that a high school friend of mine became a police chief in Seoul. I called him up. I congratulated him on being promoted to such a high position, and then I explained that I wanted him to help me in finding the biological parents of an adoptee in the United States. His answer was very simple: "Hey, Wooj, do you know how many people live in Korea today? More than fifty-five million. The city of Seoul alone has more than twenty million people. I would guess there would be more than one hundred thousand people sharing the same names as Anna's parents. Forget about it."

I knew he was right, but I wrote a sincere, yet logical, letter to him. I wrote: "Dear Chief Kim, This is pursuant to our telephone conversation we had a couple of weeks ago. If Anna was born in 1979, and suppose her parents were embarrassingly young back then, say about sixteen or nineteen years old, then today her parents would be about forty-six to forty-nine years old this year. I heard you have access to a national database. Can you somehow find people with the names of Hyun Soo Lee and Young Hee Lee and narrow them down to the age group of forty-six to forty-nine? I will buy you dinner when I see you in Seoul next time. Sincerely, Wooj."

In a few days, I received an email from Chief Kim. In it he

wrote: "Wooj, you are crazy. But I will do it for you anyway. I will do it on one condition. You don't buy me dinner. As a public servant, I cannot take a bribe. When you come to Seoul, I will buy you dinner."

I shared this exciting news with Anna, but she was trying to control her feelings this time. Understandably, she was still disappointed at the mismatching DNA test in 2006.

It was either June or July of 2007 that I received another email from Chief Kim in Seoul. He said he could narrow the list down to one hundred women and three hundred men who might possibly be Anna's parents. And he asked me what to do with this list.

I responded: "Dear Chief Kim: This may sound crazy, and I know that you think I am crazy anyway. Can you possibly call them up? Each of them! And ask whether they gave up a girl by the name of Min Joo Lee to Minnesota about twenty-eight years ago? I bet one of them will say yes."

Chief Kim responded: "Wooj, now you really are crazy. I hope you know that. It may take another three to four months. Now I change my mind. Next time you come to Korea, you have to buy me dinner."

In December of 2007, Chief Kim informed me that none of the men he contacted even acknowledged they had a child. I said it was understandable. Then he said he somehow managed to narrow down the list to ten women who all appeared to be very good candidates as Anna's biological mother.

Without a moment's hesitation, I asked Anna to pull another fifty strands of her hair for a second DNA test. On December 24, 2007, I received an email from Chief Kim: "Dear Wooj, I have good news for you. One lady's DNA matched Anna's 99.99999997 percent. Scientists never say 100 percent, but we policemen usually call this 100 percent. I am attaching a few photos of her. You will see Anna is a spitting image of this woman."

I forwarded the email to Anna. At this news, finally, Anna was happy. The pain I felt around Christmas 2006 turned into joy exactly one year later!

On June 26, 2008, Anna went to Korea to meet with her mother. Chief Kim provided a police officer to interpret the conversation between Anna and her Korean mother. As soon as Anna came back to Minnesota, she came to my office to thank me. She gave me a photo of her mother and herself, which was taken in a restaurant in Seoul.

In February 2009, Anna and her husband went to Korea again to meet her mother. Soon after, Anna sent me an email. She wrote: "Dear Wooj, Thank you so much for helping me to find my biological mother. Now I can start my own family and tell my children where their mother came from. Thanks to your help, I actually discovered two people—my mother and myself. You know what? This experience was almost like finding a new world. Sincerely, Anna."

In August 2010, I received another email from Anna, who informed me that she gave birth to a beautiful baby boy. I am looking forward to meeting this new person in her family. I also hope that this boy can meet with his Korean grandmother sometime in the future.

Hanbok Bank

The trouble about man is twofold: he cannot learn truths
which are too complicated; he forgets truths which are too
simple.

—Rebecca West

A friend of mine used to boast about his investment in Washington
Mutual. He tripled his money in a very short period of time (which
made me envious, naturally), but in an equally short time, he lost
all his money when Washington Mutual went bankrupt. Contrary
to the public's belief that banks are the safest place to keep money,
in the early 2000s, we saw many banks, such as IndyMac and
Lehman Brothers, as well as Washington Mutual, going bankrupt.
Between 2008 and 2009 alone, as many as three thousand small-
and medium-sized banks shut their business in the United States.
In the middle of this frenzy of giant corporate bankruptcies, I was
bold and crazy enough to open a bank. When I told my friends and
neighbors that I would open a bank, nobody believed me, but I
somehow managed to open one. Here is the story.

Anna Anderson told me that the hanbok (a traditional and
colorful Korean costume) she received from me provided her with a

lot of comfort and hope until we succeeded in finding her biological mother in Korea. She said to me one day that it would be great if other adoptees from Korea had a hanbok, as well. So I began to explore the possibility. And one day, the concept of "Hanbok Bank" dawned on me.

In January 2008, when the headlines of daily newspapers were flooded with the bankruptcy of financial institutions around the world, I launched a bank. By not having any money and not knowing where to hire people anyway, I decided to appoint myself as the CEO, managing director, export/import agent, and also the only clerk of this new institution that I titled "Hanbok Bank." I received donated hanboks from Korea, and then distributed them among adopted Koreans in Minnesota at one dollar per hanbok. Everyone told me this is a good price. Hanboks sell at around $150 to $1,500 per piece, depending on the quality. Even though it lacked a building or "bankers," Hanbok Bank has been doing fairly well, in the sense that it always has a sufficient reserve to satisfy the customers, unlike banks such as IndyMac or Washington Mutual or Lehman Brothers, who all went out of business because they could not meet the demands of customers with their cash reserve.

In contrast to adoptees from China, Romania, Guatemala, and Vietnam, most of whom are still relatively young today, many Korean adoptees have already become adults. I heard that in the 1970s and 1980s, there was a period of time when the only available international orphans were from Korea. When these Korean adoptees became teenagers or adults, many of them suddenly realized they looked different from their adopting parents or siblings, who were, in the case of Minnesota, mostly descendants of European countries, such as Sweden or Norway. When they realized that they were not Scandinavians, they asked their parents: "Dad, Mom, where did I come from? Do I have another set of parents?" I heard some parents tell their adopted kids that they came from heaven or they were gifts from God. That may be a good answer for young children, but it's not a practical one when the adoptees become aware of their heritage as young adults. Not satisfied with their parents' response, the adoptees soon began to look around for a different or better answer. These adopted Koreans, who are seeking their identities, have become the customers of my "Hanbok Bank."

Hanbok is the traditional Korean dress. It is often characterized by vibrant colors and simple lines without pockets. Although the term literally means "Korean clothing," hanbok today often refers specifically to hanbok of the Joseon (Chosön) period and is worn as semiformal or formal wear during traditional festivals and celebrations. It is usually worn by Koreans on major holidays, such as New Year's Day, Thanksgiving (better known as Full Moon Day in Korea), and one's own birthday. Traditional women's hanboks consist of *jeogori*, a blouse shirt or a jacket, and *chima*, a wrap-around skirt. The ensemble is often called *chima jeogori*. Men's hanboks consist of *jeogori* and *baji*, which means *pants* in Korea. The *baji* were baggy pants in traditional men's hanboks.

I met many adoptees and their family members who wanted to purchase a hanbok, but they didn't know where or how to order one. Knowing these folks' dilemma, I decided that it made sense to bring hanboks from Korea and have them available when they needed one. I sent emails to friends and relatives in Korea asking to send me hanboks that they had at home. Many of them said it was a fantastic idea, but not many actually took the painstaking job of cleaning, wrapping, and going to the post office to send one to me. One day, however, I received an email from a high school student in Seoul, who said he and his friends would help. At last, my prayer was answered. I received as many as two hundred hanboks from these high school students. Other people followed suit, and hanboks began to occupy almost half of my office space.

Since then, I have received more than four hundred hanboks and distributed them to adoptees in Minnesota. Usually the adopted Koreans came to my office to get one. Some came to my office alone. Some came with their family members. Sometimes the adoptees came with their entire family to our home and tried on the hanboks before choosing the best one for them.

This photo was taken right after Jennifer and I were married on
May 22, 1993. Koreans always wear hanboks to celebrate important moments in their lives, including their wedding ceremony.
Since I opened Hanbok Bank, I collected hundreds of hanboks,
mostly from Korea, and distributed them among adopted Koreans in Minnesota. Both graceful and colorful, the hanbok is very
popular among adopted Korean children in the United States.

Mrs. Hilary Aspen and her three children, all adopted from Korea, came to visit my office. I showed them hundreds of hanboks before they chose their favorite ones. They wanted to pay me more, but I said one dollar would be sufficient. They suggested they take a family photo of them all wearing hanboks and that I use the image to promote the business. I thought it was an excellent idea.

Hanboks cost hundreds (sometimes thousands) of dollars in Korea. Since I receive them free, however, all I have to charge my customers is one dollar per hanbok. This one dollar helps me bring more hanboks from Korea in return. As long as there are people who need hanboks (demand), and as long as there are people who send me hanboks (supply), this bank will be in business. With both sufficient reserve and sufficient customers, the future of this bank looks bright. Most recently, a ten-year-old girl, called Emma, and her father, named Jeff, came to my office and purchased a hanbok, which she needed for her dance performance at school. I said one dollar will do, but Jeff gave me twenty-five dollars for Emma's hanbok, saying that he wants me to continue this bank. I said I would. With Jeff's money of twenty-five dollars, now I can bring more hope from Korea.

As the CEO of Hanbok Bank, I may not have the kind of perks given to the CEOs of Washington Mutual or Lehman Brothers. But the joy I derive from this bank's business is priceless. I would never trade my job for one with a big bank.

Hee Ah Lee:
The Four-Fingered Pianist

I don't think there's any richer reward in life than helping
someone. You don't measure it in money or fame or
anything else. But if we're not put here for anything else
but to help each other get through life, I think that's very
honorable existence.

—Tom Brokaw

Rotary stands for "service above self." I am not always good at it,
but I try to live up to that spirit by getting involved in as many
charitable activities as possible. One such activity includes the Korean Culture Camp at Minnehaha Academy in Minneapolis. This
camp is designed for children adopted from Korea, who want to
learn about their heritage. I have participated in this camp as both
a teacher and a volunteer parent. My two daughters have been frequent participants in this camp, as well.

   At this camp in July 2007, as usual, I sat on a bench to enjoy the performance of the campers, which usually takes place at
the end of the week-long camp. There was a program during which
young children (six or seven years old) held each other's hands,
sang, and danced. For some reason, the circle did not form, and it

didn't take much time for the audience to realize why. There was a boy whose arms were too short, and his hands each had only one finger. It was obvious the kids next to him were too scared to hold his hands. Realizing he could not participate in the program in any meaningful way, despite his willingness, the boy sadly turned around and ran to his mother in the audience. To this day, I cannot forget the image of the shocking scene and the boy's frustrated face. The audience quickly forgot this sad drama, however, because other colorful events soon followed. The camp ended successfully, but my head was full of questions about the boy: How is he going to live with only one finger on each hand? How can I possibly help him? Why did his parents adopt him of all the possible eligible orphans?

After the camp was over, I went back to the busy routine of my daily life. Then one day in April 2008, I happened to see a pianist on YouTube. Her performance was so uplifting and blissful that it brought tears to my eyes. But then, all of a sudden, I felt a slap to my face when I quickly realized that the pianist had only two fingers on each hand. I immediately thought that it would be awesome if the boy in the camp could meet this musician!

Without wasting a moment, I contacted all my friends and relatives to find out who this pianist was. I discovered her name was Hee Ah Lee, and she was quite a celebrity in South Korea already. I also contacted the summer camp director and teachers to reach the boy, but I realized the camp would not disclose information about him for privacy reasons. I could not learn the boy's whereabouts or name.

Realizing that I might not be able to locate the boy, I almost gave up this project. But a few people encouraged me to go forward. As a matter of fact, two members of Edina Rotary Club (Joel Jennings and Ted Yock) approached me and each gave me one thousand dollars as seed money. Jongwoo Kim, a friend of mine in Korea, also sent me one thousand dollars and encouraged me to continue with this project. After locating Hee Ah Lee, I explained the reason why she should come to Minnesota. I told her there were many special people in Minnesota who all wanted to meet with her, including a boy who shared her physical condition. To my relief and joy, Hee Ah Lee agreed to come.

I contacted virtually all of the theaters in Minnesota and discovered Hopkins High School Auditorium had the largest capacity for people with disabilities, which, I thought, would work well for our target audience. The city council of Hopkins made a resolution to declare October 19, 2008, to be "Hee Ah Lee Day," and Mr. Eugene Maxwell, the mayor of Hopkins, issued a certificate to that effect.

More than five hundred people attended Hee Ah Lee's concert. To my delight, the boy (I later discovered that his name was Michael) showed up with all of his family members. His father thanked me for making such efforts for his son. I thanked him for coming to the concert. During the intermission, at least two children who shared the pianist's physical condition came forward. Some even suggested creating a medical foundation for those suffering from the condition. I later discovered that this condition is known as focomelia, and it causes malformation of the arms, legs, fingers, toes, or ears.

I didn't expect it to happen, but Hee Ah Lee's performance in Minnesota was covered not only by the local newspapers, such as the *Sun Current* and the *Star Tribune*, but it was covered by TV stations, such as CNN and MSNBC, as well, and Hee Ah Lee became famous all around the world.

I received a phone call from Hee Ah Lee in December 2008, two months after her inspirational performance in Minnesota.

"Mr. Byun, do you know where I am?" she began. "I am performing in Mexico this week, and I will perform in China next month. Because of your hard work, and also because of CNN's coverage of my performance in Minnesota, many Mexicans recognize me already. I want to thank you."

I wrote an email back to her:

Dear Hee Ah:

It was good to hear your voice again. You are an angel, and you always sound wonderful. It was my honor to meet

71

an international performer like you here in Minnesota. I have good news for you. Michael, the boy who was inspired by you, is playing guitar with his two fingers. You sowed the seeds of hope in him and hundreds of other people who have physical handicaps like you. I am glad you are performing in Mexico and China. You will inspire hundreds of thousands of people there, too. Please remember that our hearts always follow and stay with you. Let's keep in touch.

Sincerely, Wooj.

Hee Ah Lee came to Minnesota all the way from Korea, mainly to inspire Michael, a six-year-old boy, but she ended up inspiring tens of thousands of other people. With only two fingers on each hand, and without legs under her kneecaps, she may have been born as a most unfortunate person on earth; however, she taught us how to live with a most positive attitude.

After she left Minnesota, I realized the power of Internet. The Human Rights Commission in the Netherlands contacted me, after watching Hee Ah Lee's performance in Minnesota on the Internet. They wanted to invite her to inspire handicapped people in the Netherlands. Without a moment's hesitation, I conveyed this message to Hee Ah and highly recommended she go there. After a successful performance in the Netherlands in early 2009, where she was widely welcomed by all the Dutch people, Hee Ah Lee received an award from the Human Rights Commission of the Netherlands for giving hope and inspiration to all Dutch people with disabilities.

Michael's family and our family became good friends. With her extraordinary piano performance, Hee Ah Lee connected many people to one another.

This photo was taken after Hee Ah Lee's Minnesota concert in 2008. Michael, Hee Ah, and I all became good friends.

Mr. Rocky, Peter Jennings, and a Liquor License

> When a man realizes his littleness, his greatness can appear.
> —H.G. Wells

Have you ever been to a city council meeting? I highly recommend that you go to one if you haven't yet. You will appreciate the fact that there are many people who try to steer the city in the right direction by sacrificing their sleep for the best interest of their fellow citizens. If you watch a city council meeting for just five minutes, you will be comfortably assured that you are in good hands. If America is a great country, I think it is because of city council meetings, where grassroots citizens freely express their opinions, and the city council members work hard to reflect the citizens' opinions on the city's business.

Ms. Shin had been saving money to open a restaurant. Since she came to the United States as a teenager, she had always had two or three jobs at a time in order to save money. Perhaps because she was spending too much time working, her married life was not very smooth. She married three times, and each resulted in divorce. From each marriage, she had one child. Even though the children had different fathers, they were on good terms with each other and were very supportive of their mother.

As soon as Ms. Shin decided that she had enough money, she quit her jobs and purchased a restaurant in a small city called Cambridge Valley (the name of the city has been changed). She hired a manager. As she spent weeks with the manager drafting a business plan, purchasing necessary equipment, and developing menus, the two fell in love and decided to get married soon after opening the new restaurant.

For the first sixty days, they could use the previous owner's liquor license; however, toward the end of this initial sixty days of ownership transition, the city required a new application from Ms. Shin. When the city council discovered that Ms. Shin and her husband were not United States citizens, it demanded a hearing to determine the couple's eligibility for the new liquor license.

At eight p.m. on August 31, 2001, Ms. Shin, her husband, and I all went to the city hall to attend the city council meeting. There were five council members who had at least one hundred items on their agenda before Ms. Shin's liquor license hearing. It was my first time attending such a meeting. To our surprise, there were many people from the community who came to express their opinions either for or against the liquor license application Ms. Shin submitted.

It was almost midnight when our case was finally heard.

The mayor said, "Item number 107. Liquor license application submitted by Ms. Ok Soon Shin through her attorney, Mr. Byun. Ms. Shin and Mr. Byun, please come forward and tell us why we should give you a liquor license."

I went to the podium with Ms. Shin and said, "Mr. Mayor and honorable members of the city council, Ms. Shin purchased this restaurant from the previous owner about two months ago. As you know, this restaurant has done very well over the past thirty years, and it always served liquor to its customers. If the previous owner was given a liquor license, then my client should be given a license, as well. Ms. Shin has been waiting for this moment all her life. She saved money to purchase and renovate the restaurant, obtained a food handler's license to launch the restaurant business, and now she wants to continue to serve wine and beer to her customers. She will honor the terms and conditions of the liquor license, if given to her by the city."

Mr. Rocky, the oldest and seemingly wisest member of the council, leaned forward to speak into the microphone and said, "Counsel, it appears to me that Ms. Shin is not a United States citizen. In addition, it appears that her husband was illegal in this country at one point. I feel very uncomfortable allowing a liquor license in the hands of an illegal foreigner."

After Mr. Rocky made his point, the mayor gave permission for the citizens to express their views. Two groups of people lined up and began speaking from both corners of the city council chamber. One group agreed with Mr. Rocky and spoke mainly about possible abuse of the license. They were worried about increased crime rates because of alcohol consumption. Some pointed out recent increases in criminal cases, such as DWIs or homicides, which were all related to alcohol abuse. Many of them were long-time residents and were genuinely worried about the license's potential abuse that could result in a bad reputation for their city and decreased property values. I developed a lot of respect for these folks' willingness to sacrifice their sleep and come to the city hall to share their concerns.

The other group was composed mostly of recent immigrants. One person, who identified himself as an Italian immigrant, said, "Councilman Rocky, Americans all came from somewhere. I may be an Italian immigrant, but I am a proud American. This Korean couple will eventually become American citizens. You should give the liquor license to them." A few other citizens also presented their opinion similar to this Italian gentleman.

Mr. Rocky was not impressed by these immigrants, and he would not change his mind. He said, "My grandfather and father used to go to this restaurant. I went there, too. The owners of this restaurant have always been responsible United States citizens, as far as I remember. We cannot take this liquor license issue lightly. Innocent citizens could become victims of alcohol-related crimes. I cannot approve this application."

After spending a good sixty minutes or so discussing what "a good United States citizen" means, and why the new applicants should or should not be trusted any less than their previous counterparts, I decided to speak one more time.

"Mr. Rocky, from the documents we submitted to you, you know that Ms. Shin applied for United States citizenship already, and her husband is going to receive his green card very soon."

"But she is not a United States citizen yet. That's what counts here," Mr. Rocky said matter-of-factly.

"Okay. Then, Mr. Rocky, have you heard of people like Paul Shaffer, Peter Jennings, or Mike Wallace?"

"What about them? What do they have to do with this liquor license application?" Mr. Rocky asked in a most puzzled way.

"With all due respect, I want you to answer me for now. Have you ever seen or heard of them?"

"Yes, I have seen them on TV," a confused Mr. Rocky said.

"Mr. Rocky, do you know what they have in common?" I asked.

"Counsel, I don't know what you are talking about. I don't know, and I don't care," Mr. Rocky said in an irritated way.

"Let me tell you what they have in common. They are all Canadians. They are not US citizens. Let's suppose Mr. Peter Jennings came here to apply for liquor license. Or Paul Shaffer. Or Mike Wallace. Mr. Rocky, would you have treated them exactly the same way as you are treating Ms. Shin or her husband? Ms. Shin is a green card holder. So is Peter Jennings. So is Mike Wallace. So is Paul Shaffer. As a matter of fact, Ms. Shin already submitted a US citizenship application to the immigration office, which these Canadians did not and would not. I strongly believe Ms. Shin is entitled to the same amount of respect and consideration from you, if not more."

Clearly irritated, Mr. Rocky shouted, "Counsel, it is incredible that Peter Jennings is not a US citizen. Well, I don't think Peter Jennings or his wife would apply for a liquor license here in our city, anyhow. Besides, I don't think Peter Jennings or his wife would have been illegal in this country. In any event, I don't think a liquor license should be given to a non-United States citizen! Period! That's my view."

The clock was now indicating almost one o'clock in the morning, but nobody would leave the room. Realizing that we may not reach a tangible result this way, the mayor kicked in, finally. "Mr. Byun, you made your point well. Mr. Rocky, we heard your opinion very well, too. I appreciate all the citizens who came here tonight to share their views. Ms. Shin, thanks for applying for a liquor license in our city. In the interest of everyone's sleeping time, I suggest that we cast our vote on this issue now. Those in favor say aye. Those against say nay."

Only Mr. Rocky cast a nay vote. All the other council members, including the mayor, approved Ms. Shin's liquor license application.

The mayor continued, "The motion is carried. Ms. Shin, congratulations on the approval of your liquor license application. I'd like to visit your restaurant one of these days. I wish you and your business great success in the future. We welcome you in our city. You may go home now."

Ms. Shin and her husband were holding each other in tears and could not thank the mayor enough. Their supporters, including the Italian gentleman, were all embracing the couple. I felt all choked up inside.

I still wonder if Mr. Rocky would have said no if people like Peter Jennings or Mike Wallace or Paul Shaffer, along with their Canadian spouses, came to the city hall meeting to obtain a liquor license. Maybe he would have still casted a nay vote if he is a consistent man.

Some time later, Ms. Shin called me. She said, "Mr. Byun, as far as I am concerned, you are the best lawyer in the world. I became a US citizen a few weeks ago, and my husband will receive his green card soon. I am pregnant, and we will have a new baby early next year. I hope you can come to our restaurant some time and enjoy a beer with us."

I genuinely felt good. It was one of the happiest and proudest moments throughout my entire career as a lawyer.

China Boy Singing
an Irish Song!

When you plant lettuce, if it does not grow well, you don't
blame the lettuce. You look for reasons it is not doing
well. It may need fertilizer, or more water or less sun. You
never blame the lettuce. Yet if we have problems with our
friends or family, we blame the other person. But if we
know how to take care of them, they will grow well, like
the lettuce. Blaming has no positive effect at all. . . . No
blame, no reasoning, no argument, just understanding. If
you understand, and you show that you understand, you
can love, and the situation will change.

—Thich Nhat Hanh

Every time I waited for our two daughters' piano lessons to finish at
Saint Joseph's School of Music, I just felt totally useless. Sometimes
I read a newspaper or took a nap while sitting on the bench in
the lobby, but either way, I was bored. I wished I were learning
something practical or useful during that waiting time, instead of
just sitting around and doing nothing for two hours. One day, as
usual, I was at the music academy, feeling exactly the same way,
when I happened to see a man sitting alone in a room across from

my daughter's classroom. Out of curiosity, I quietly said hi to him and asked what he was doing alone in an empty classroom.

He said, "I am a teacher here, and I'm waiting for my next student to show up. Today two students cancelled their classes, and that means I have to teach only one student. He will show up in one hour. So I am getting ready for him."

I asked him, "What do you teach?"

He said, "I teach saxophone. Unlike other instruments, such as piano or violin or cello, there are not many students who want to learn saxophone. With so few students, I am not sure how much longer I can teach here. I need more students to make ends meet."

So I began to take saxophone lessons from him.

My teacher was a Chinese man by the name of Mr. Yi. He graduated from the famous Central Conservatory of Music in Beijing. His family immigrated to the United States, thinking that living in the United States would provide a much better educational opportunity for their two children. Since he always wore the same shirt, I somehow thought he was struggling financially, which turned out to be a wrong assumption. (I discovered later that he owned a moderately successful import/export company and also that he was financially secure.) He sold his old saxophone to me. The instrument was not in the best condition, but it was good enough for someone like me, who just started to take lessons. Most of the time he had only four to five students for the entire month. This small number of students helped him earn barely enough money to cover his transportation expenses. What made me respect him was that he was always happy, in spite of the small number of students he had. He told me he had started importing musical instruments, such as violins and violas, from China to supplement his income.

Then an incident happened which changed the course of our lives. One summer day he was not in the mood to teach, and I was not in the mood to learn. So we sneaked out of the school and went fishing at Lake Minnetonka. He told me not to report our frolic to the headmaster, Sister Mary, who was a Catholic nun. I told him it depended on how many fish we caught. As luck had it, we didn't catch any fish. Not to disappoint me, and also to make sure that I didn't report this frolic to Sister Mary, he invited me to his house, and we had a very nice Chinese dinner cooked by his wife, who was rather confused by the visit of an unannounced guest at her dinner table.

After dinner and plenty of wine, Mr. Yi told me that, even though he has never amassed any fortune with his humble music lessons, he never regretted becoming a music teacher. He also told me that he sincerely hopes that I make more friends in the future with the music he taught me. He told me that music helps us transcend all our differences. I thought he was a great man because he often sounded like a Confucius scholar.

We continued our lessons for about a year, until we both lost momentum. The lessons I took from him, however, turned out to be very useful. I played saxophone at my friends' important celebrations, such as my godfather's birthday party, and so far nobody has complained about my performance, to my relief.

Since I learned saxophone from Mr. Yi, I developed a habit of humming or whistling some of my favorite saxophone music that I learned from him, such as "Danny Boy," "Annie Laurie," and songs from *The Sound of Music*. Sometimes, while I am waiting for the traffic lights to change, I simulate playing saxophone, too. It just makes me happy.

Mr. Yi taught me a lesson, that music has the power to help us transcend all our superficial differences and bring us together, but I had one occasion when this lesson didn't work quite the way I expected. The following incident happened a few years ago, when I was serving as a board member of the Korean Service Center's family advocacy program. We had our board meetings in a Minneapolis building where many nonprofit organizations had their offices, too.

I thought I was alone. So I began to sing "Danny Boy" in front of the urinal. But quickly I discovered that there was another man in the toilet stall when I suddenly heard the flush. It was Tom, a gentleman working for another nonprofit organization in the same building. Coming out of the toilet stall, he said, "Ha! China boy singing an Irish song! How interesting!"

He washed his hands, smiled a lot, and left the bathroom, still rejoicing in his own benign remark. Both my song and urination stopped temporarily, and I resumed them very cautiously only after making sure that there was nobody else in the men's room.

During the board meeting, I could not help thinking about this incident. I didn't know Tom very well. All I knew was that he was an executive of another nonprofit organization in the building, where I bumped into him once or twice a month. He was slightly older than me. Before jumping to any conclusion about him, I thought I should get to know him better. I also thought that I should properly introduce myself to him.

So I went to his office as soon as our meeting was over. The building had fewer than twenty offices, so it was relatively easy to find Tom's office. He was a bit surprised to see me. This was the conversation I had with him:

"Tom, I came to say hi to you."

"Okay, but I am kind of busy. Shall we make it short?"

"All right. I will try. I come here for the Korean Service Center's board meeting once or twice a month. My name is Woodrow Byun. Some call me Wooj. I came originally from Korea. I worked in Hong Kong briefly before coming to the United States. I became a naturalized citizen of the United States this past year."

A bit puzzled, Tom said, "Congratulations! Glad to meet you. I am Thomas McAlister. My parents came from England originally. So you may regard me as English-American."

"Thanks for the introduction. You may remember seeing me before in this building. You may also remember seeing me in the men's room about thirty minutes ago. Do you?"

"Yes. I know you. I met you before."

"When you saw me in the bathroom, you said, 'Ha! China boy singing an Irish song.' When I heard it, to tell you the truth, it puzzled me greatly. If you said I was too loud or my voice was unbearable or something like that, then I would have understood you, and I may have seriously considered apologizing to you. But you didn't complain to me, did you? Can you tell me what you meant by saying what you did in the bathroom?"

Realizing that I didn't come just to say hi to him, Tom, quite surprised, turned his head to look outside the window and said, "I may have overheard from someone that you came from China. So I called you 'China boy.' As we all know, 'Danny Boy' is a famous song from Ireland. I thought it was interesting to hear a China boy singing 'Danny Boy.' That's all."

"All right. In that case, I am glad I came to see you. First of all, I came from Korea. So from today, you may call me a Korean boy, not a China boy, although I do not like to be called a boy anyway. But it still sounds better than a China boy. Music is an important part of my life. You may find me singing 'Danny Boy' again in the men's room or in the hallway. Next time you hear me singing or humming or whistling, please do not hesitate to let me know if I am too loud or if you cannot stand my singing voice or anything of that nature. I will stop immediately. In fact, I am thinking that I should refrain from singing in your presence from now on anyway, so it may not become an issue between the two of us. Basically, I want to peacefully coexist with you every time I come to this building or when we use men's room at the same time."

Noticing that I was clearly agitated, Tom said, "Oh, feel free to sing. This is a free country. You do whatever you want. I didn't mean to hurt your feelings by what I said in the bathroom."

I was glad to discover that he didn't mean any harm. As I left his office, I wasn't sure whether I achieved anything, but I felt slightly better after talking with him. From that day on, I always said hello to Tom, in the parking ramp or in the bathroom or in the hallway. I somehow thought avoiding him would make our relationship worse, but I was not ready or determined to become best friends with him, either. Every time I said hi, Tom usually ignored me. It was obvious he didn't feel very comfortable about the conversation we had regarding the bathroom encounter.

About two years passed. Maybe saying hi diligently to Tom

paid off because he began to be friendly with me. For whatever reason, we are on much better terms now, and we always say hi to each other. Sometimes I wonder if Tom will ever sing a Chinese song in the men's room. And if that happens, I wonder if I should say to him, "Ha! An England man sings a Chinese song in the bathroom! How interesting!" I wonder if Tom would become agitated at my comment. Somehow I have the feeling it will not happen during our lifetimes.

My saxophone teacher taught me that music is a universal language that can unite people of different cultures and backgrounds. In a way, Mr. Yi's lesson holds true even with the relationship between Tom and me. Were it not for that encounter in the men's room where I sang "Danny Boy" as a China boy, I don't think Tom and I would have had the chance to become friends. Thank you, Mr. Yi, for the lesson. Because of you, I met a wonderful English-American man, and we became good friends with each other. Music is great. It connects people to each other.

Money and Happiness

What money can buy:
A bed but not sleep
Computer but not brain
Food but not appetite
Finery but not beauty
A house but not a home
Medicine but not health
Luxuries but not culture
Amusements but not happiness
Acquaintance but not friends
Obedience but not faithfulness
Sex but not love

　　　　　　　　—Anonymous

According to a recent poll conducted by the website *Daum*, Koreans define a "wealthy person" as "someone with an asset of more than two million US dollars." I like the simplicity of this definition. It is black or white, and under this definition, by examining just a few financial documents, you can easily tell who is wealthy and who is not. While I participated in the Rotary International convention in New Orleans in 2011, I had a chance to speak with a group of French Rotarians about what makes a person wealthy. A Rotarian from Paris gave me a rather sophisticated and interesting definition of a wealthy person in France: "A wealthy person is someone who can speak at least one foreign language, play one or more musical instruments, cook and invite friends to share the cooked food, has the means to travel whenever he wants, has the courage to scold someone else's child, and is willing to discuss social justice and participate in it."

When I heard the French definition the first time, I became numb, as if a hammer hit my head. Interestingly enough, it allows those who have a modest income to be regarded as wealthy, too. In other words, under this definition, you don't have to struggle to meet a certain quantified threshold, such as two million dollars, to be called wealthy. Instead, all you need to do is cook some meals and share them with friends to become wealthy. By virtue of learning a foreign language and musical instruments, you become wealthy. The more I think about it, the more I like this definition.

Sometimes I think a wealthy Korean man and his counterpart in France should trade their lives for just one month. That way, they can find out whether they are truly wealthy, regardless of their socio-cultural environment. At the end of the exchanged month, they may come back, scratching their heads, and say, "Gee, I was not wealthy in that strange country." Or they may say, "Before this trade, I didn't realize how truly wealthy I was." Either way, I am sure they will learn something new from each other.

Years ago, I saw a special program on ABC, titled *Happiness*. John Stossel, the host with a stylish beard, interviewed two groups of people. One group was composed of twenty individuals who each won more than twenty million dollars in the lottery, and the other group was composed of a bunch of Amish women. Mr. Stossel interviewed and compared these two groups to find out the relationship between money and happiness.

Somehow I had been under the impression that those who won lottery money would be wildly happy, but, to my surprise, according to the TV program, as many as sixteen people out of the twenty who received millions of dollars were divorced after winning the jackpot, developed bad habits, such as alcoholism or gambling, and were most unhappy after their initial and short-lived euphoria. By contrast, a group of Amish women, who had little money but plenty of friendly cousins and neighbors, were too busy to become unhappy. Some Amish women had lost their husbands or children to cancer or accidents, but the result was the same—they were still happy. The conclusion of the program was that ownership of material things didn't necessarily guarantee happiness.

After watching this program, I began to wonder: What is this concept we call "ownership," anyway? Is there any relationship between what I own and what I become? For example, if I owned a Rolex watch, do I become a better money manager? If I lived in the biggest or most luxurious house in my neighborhood, am I the best citizen in my neighborhood? If I owned the most expensive car, am I the best driver? If I live in this world only a brief period of time, and if my body, mind, and all the material things I own are transitory and recycled eventually, can I truly say I own them permanently?

Joe Christiansen, a Rotarian friend of mine, once said, "When I didn't have much money, I could say I owned it, but as I accumulated more, I realized that money began to own me." This was very similar to my father's thought on alcohol. My father used to tell me, "Son, you should not drink. At the beginning, you consume alcohol; but after a while, alcohol begins to consume you. That's why we should not drink. In fact, there are many things in this world you should abstain from because they tend to own and control you unless you control them wisely."

People in today's world have the tendency to own (or want to own) more, even though they know that ownership creates more problems than happiness. About six years ago, I got to know a couple who became most unhappy because of a large amount of money that came as a gift. It started when I received a phone call from a man, named Tim, in a rural county jail. He sounded very desperate. He said he was wrongly accused and jailed. I didn't like the idea of having to pay the hefty cost of collect calls from the jail, but at least I wanted to find out what this man named Tim had to say so desperately. Here is his story:

Tim and his wife, Ange, were both from Korea. They had a humble but steady retail business in a rural town in Minnesota. Their only problem was they had no children. Finally, after ten years of expensive in vitro sessions, they managed to produce a son.

Strangely enough, it was Tim's father in Korea who was happier than Tim about this birth. Both Tim and Ange had been under a lot of pressure from their family in Korea to produce an heir. In many Asian countries, it is still true that when a woman marries the eldest son of a family, one of her primary duties is to produce a male offspring. In this case, with this grandson's birth, Tim's father was totally relieved and extremely happy. He expressed his gratitude to the young couple by sending a gift of two hundred thousand dollars in cash.

Up until that moment, the couple was poor yet happy, but with this large sum of money wire-transferred from Korea, troubles began to brew. Both Tim and Ange used to be Buddhists in Korea, but in Minnesota they began to go to church. After attending church for more than ten years, Ange learned the importance of the tithe, and when the cash gift came, she assumed 10 percent (or twenty thousand dollars) should go to their church. Tim, however, had a slightly different opinion. He argued that this was a gift, not income. Ange became angry. She said to Tim, "Regardless of the source, any money coming into this household is *income*, and we pay a tithe based on our *income*. Period."

Tim called his father to determine the nature of the money. His father told him, "It was a *gift* to be used for your son's welfare and education, and, therefore, no part should go to the church. Tell your wife what I just told you."

Unable to resolve this issue in a civilized fashion, the couple somehow escalated their argument into a fistfight. Ange ended up calling the police, and Tim was arrested when he was about to strangle Ange out of extreme fury.

When I went to the arraignment (the first appearance of the defendant in a criminal case), I discovered that Ange had already filed a no-contact temporary restraining order and also a divorce lawsuit against Tim. Tim was devastated. He just wanted to get out of jail as soon as possible and go back to the old days when he was happy with Ange and their newborn son. However, the judge didn't allow Tim to contact Ange anymore, because, according to the judge, Tim still posed a threat to the safety of his family.

The parties' divorce became final within the next few months. Tim lost virtually everything as a result of the divorce. He lost almost all of his money, including his father's gift, as well as the business and the valuable items in their house. Their son's temporary custody was awarded to Ange. He had tremendous regret. Were it not for the cash gift from his father, Tim and Ange may be still married to each other. Ultimately, Tim thought that he was punished for not honoring and respecting his wife's wish to pay the tithe.

On another occasion, I came across a dying person who had saved a large amount of money, which ended up helping a young man start a new life. It happened in the winter of 2002, when I was serving as a board member of the Korean Association of Minnesota. I received a phone call from Dr. Murphy of Hennepin County Medical Center. There was something urgent in his voice.

He said, "Mr. Byun, can you come to the Hennepin County Medical Center Emergency Room? We have a dying man here, and we need your help."

When I rushed to the emergency room, Mr. Kim, president of Korean Association, was speaking with Dr. Murphy, who said the patient had no chance of living. According to Dr. Murphy, the Korean man had had a major stroke, and because no one discovered him until almost half a day later, the hospital missed the opportunity to save him. His brain was dead already, but he was still breathing.

Now the pressing questions were: Who had the right to end his life by removing the lifeline from his mouth? Did he have any family here? Mr. Kim told me the man was found in front of a restaurant early in the morning. Apparently, he was the last patron to leave the restaurant, and he fell as soon as he stepped out of the restaurant the previous evening. His fallen body was quickly covered by the snow. He was not found until the morning after. Nobody knew who he was, and he had no identification on him.

With help from the Minneapolis police, we discovered his name was J. R. Hong, and he was fifty-eight years old. He was in the United States illegally. Apparently, he had lost a job in Korea several years before, and he had left his family and came to America to seek better employment. After working at several construction sites in New York, he realized that the high living expenses there didn't allow him to save at all. So he decided to come to Minnesota, and in the next two years, he managed to save some money. But he totally ignored his health problems while saving money, and, finally, he had a stroke.

With help from the Korean Consulate Office in Chicago, we found out that Mr. Hong had a son in Korea, the only relative we could actually contact. The son was in high school and was staying with a remote relative. Because he was only seventeen years old, however, he could not make any decision about his father's vegetative condition.

Dr. Murphy turned to us. "Mr. Kim and Mr. Byun, you two gentlemen decide Mr. Hong's fate. As I told you, he has no chance to live. His vegetative state may continue for several months, but in the meantime, his body cells will die gradually. You may like to talk to his family in Korea, but as you are the only connection we have as far as we are concerned, we want you to make the decision. Minnesota law does not allow the hospital to make a decision to terminate a patient's life. The decision should come from the patient's family or representative."

About this time, we found his apartment in Minneapolis. He was living in a house along with six other construction workers. To our surprise, the other tenants didn't seem to know Mr. Hong very well. When we entered his room, we were shocked to see that he owned almost nothing. The only things we could find were a suitcase with basic clothing items in it. In the suitcase, however, we also found a small box that contained a handwritten note and a bundle of dollar bills, bound by rubber band, which amounted to a total of about $15,500. The note, pencil-written on an odd-shaped piece of paper, read:

Dear My Son:

    I did my best to save money, but I could save only what you will see in the box. I just hope that whoever finds this money will honestly send it to you so that you can use it when you go to college.

Son, I want you to study hard and I want you to find a good job. Throughout my entire life, I have been a construction worker. Construction is a good job. I don't hate my job. But it has been an unstable job for me. Son, you may remember when the economic crisis came to hit Asia in 1997. That's when I lost my job. Up until then, your mother and I were very happy.

I want you to study more and become a professional. I want you to become a medical doctor or a lawyer, or something like that, so that you will never lose your job, no matter what happens to the economy.

I have the feeling that I will not be with you when you enter a college. That thought makes me sad, but I will be proud of you wherever I may be. You know no one in our family ever went to college, but I know you will be the first one in our family's history.

I know this is not much, but I hope this is useful when you go to college. I hope you forgive your mother and me. Son, please remember that I love you dearly. As I write this letter to you, I feel most happy and peaceful.

Take care of yourself.
With love, Dad

Tears streamed down our faces. We knew it was our duty to send this last letter to Mr. Hong's son in Korea, along with the saved money. We phoned Mr. Hong's son. I could tell he was crying on the other end of the line as I read his father's letter to him. I explained there was no chance of his father recovering, and I told him we should let his father leave this world with dignity. It took some time, but he agreed with me. When I informed him that his father had saved about $15,500, he was relieved because he needed to pay his first year of college tuition.

When we met Dr. Murphy again the next day, we told him of Mr. Hong's letter and also of the phone conversation we had with Mr. Hong's son. Dr. Murphy was deeply touched by the letter. He asked us to sign the consent form, according to which Mr. Hong's life would end peacefully and with dignity. When I looked at Mr. Hong's face during his final moment, he looked as if he was in peace, although I knew it was just my imagination.

Mr. Hong impacted all of us. Someone who owned so little was still able to help his son pay his first year of college tuition. When we put together his belongings to mail them to his son in Korea, they all fit inside a small cardboard box. I felt sad that a human being's ultimate belongings could be reduced to such a small box, but I also thought to myself that in a way, Mr. Hong was a happy man. He owned very little, and, therefore, he didn't have to fight with anyone in this world for more ownership. I was sure his soul, being light enough, would have gone to heaven directly and effortlessly.

One of the lottery winners on the TV program gave a very wise piece of advice: "When you hear the news that you hit the jackpot, don't even think about touching the money. Close your eyes and ears. Just donate it to a charity. The moment it enters your life, you and your family members will have lots of trouble. It could destroy your family. It could destroy your life. The choice is yours." Sometimes I wonder if someone should create a reality TV program in which millionaires and Amish people swap their lives for just one week, and then share their experience with the TV viewers. It would be interesting.

We live in an age where we are confused between convenience and happiness. Let's remember that money can buy only convenience, not happiness.

In 2006 my parents made a donation to Seoul National University Foundation. My two sisters, their husbands, and I are all alumni of Seoul National University. We visited President Un-Chan Chung's office.

From left to right: Woomin Byun (my brother), Moonwon Kang (my brother-in-law), Jumdon Hwang (my mother), Maria Byun (our second daughter), Nakmoon Byun (my father), President Chung, me, Nina Byun (our first daughter), Sook-Kyung Byun (my elder sister), and Jiwon Byun (my younger sister)

Courtroom Diversity:
How Not to Look Like a Felon

The man who has no money is poor, but one who has nothing but money is poorer. He only is rich who can enjoy without owning; he is poor who is covetous. There are riches of intellect, and no man with an intellectual taste can be called poor. He is rich as well as brave who can face compulsory poverty and misfortune with cheerfulness and courage.

—Orison Marden

In May 2012, I went to my niece's law school graduation ceremony. She finished an LLM program, which is a one-year master's program in law. At Mariucci Arena, University of Minnesota, there were about 220 JD (three-year program) students and as many as 49 LLM (one-year program) students who came to the graduation ceremony. Senator Al Franken was the guest speaker. Dean Whipmann, distinguished professors, and staff were all there, too. Members at the law school did a wonderful job of grooming the students into future lawyers and legal scholars. I noticed that more than 50 percent of JD students came from out of state or from other countries. LLM students were 100 percent from overseas. Overall, more than 60 percent of students came from out of Minnesota, and more than 20 percent came from overseas.

University of Minnesota was established more than one hundred years ago. When the law program was launched, the primary goal was to produce lawyers the state of Minnesota demanded, including legislators, lawyers in private sector, and lawyers in public sector. But today, the school turned into a global institution, where lawyers and legal scholars come from all over the world. Senator Franken emphasized the importance of pro bono work. He is right. No matter how successful they become, lawyers should always help the needy people.

As I saw my niece proudly coming down from the podium, I remembered the years I spent in this school. When I was attending the law school at the University of Minnesota two decades ago, there were only five or six students from overseas, and the majority of the student body was from Minnesota. My professors and classmates did their best to make me feel at home. But things became increasingly more difficult as soon as I became a lawyer. I found it very difficult to feel at home with people, particularly in a courtroom setting in rural parts of Minnesota, where I hardly saw lawyers of color.

Things became much better for me over time, but when I first began to practice law in 1994, often I felt very uneasy when I entered a courtroom for a court hearing. The incident I am about to relay actually happened one day when I represented a criminal defendant in a suburban Minnesota district court. My client was a Korean businessman who was charged with a felony crime for breaking into his ex-wife's house at the end of a heated telephone argument.

When my client, named Mr. Lee, called me, his voice sounded desperate. He called from the county jail, so I decided to take the case, even though I was terribly busy with other matters at that time. When I interviewed him in jail, I realized he was in a lot of trouble. I suggested that I could arrange another lawyer if he wanted, but he said he would like me to represent him, particularly because I knew him very well from working many years as his business attorney.

About one week after he was arrested, his first hearing took place. When I arrived at the court, the usual crowd was there. Well-dressed lawyers were sitting together to distinguish themselves from others. Usually they talked about the golf games they played over the weekend or an exotic fishing trip. Prosecutors, equally well dressed, looked all serious and busy with their thick court rule books and case files. Court clerks, security guards, and court reporters were talking to each other, and they all looked like a big extended family. For some mysterious reason, I didn't feel I belonged anywhere in this typical courtroom scene. So I sat with the ordinary people, who were there to attend the hearing as criminal defendants or witnesses. Since most of these criminal defendants visit the courtroom for the first time and do not know each other, they are usually quiet. Most of them have no special connection to anyone in the courtroom. Sometimes these ordinary people (including criminal defendants, suspects, witnesses, and family members) softly speak with their lawyers. Occasionally there are interpreters for people who don't speak English. I just sat at a corner with this crowd.

The judge appeared, and we all stood up. As soon as he sat down, we sat down. The clerk announced, "Case Number 2133x, Minnesota v. Mr. Lee." With that announcement, I moved to the podium across from where the judge was sitting, with Mr. Lee's files in my hand.

With a very stern voice, perfectly justified under the circumstances, the judge asked, "So, Mr. Lee, where is your lawyer?" At the beginning, I didn't know to whom he was talking. But as soon as I noticed the judge was talking to me, I said, "Your honor, I am not Mr. Lee." Before I said anything further, the judge said, "You are not Mr. Lee? Where is Mr. Lee?" At this point, everyone in the courtroom began to look around to find the felon known as Mr. Lee. I was curious, too.

I was about to explain who I was, but the clerk quickly interrupted and reported to the judge that Mr. Lee, the alleged felon, was on his way, being escorted by the police from the jail. In a matter of one or two more minutes, Mr. Lee finally showed up in a jail uniform, which was a faded blue color. His head was shaven and his hands and feet were chained.

The judge used his stern voice again toward the felon. "Let's start the hearing. Mr. Lee, do you have a lawyer?"

Mr. Lee said, "Yes."

The judge said, "I don't see any lawyer here. By the way, you can speak in your own language, Korean, if you prefer. We have an interpreter in the courtroom." At that point, I could tell the judge somehow assumed I came to the hearing as an interpreter for Mr. Lee.

Mr. Lee said, "Your Honor, I can speak English. I have spoken to my lawyer last night. He came to this room. He is right there."

Raising his chained hands, as if he was about to shoot a handgun, Mr. Lee was pointing his two index fingers at me. This time, the judge was confused.

"Who are you, gentleman? I thought you were an interpreter. Please identify yourself!" the puzzled judge said, looking at me.

I said, "Your Honor, I am Mr. Lee's lawyer. My apologies. I should have identified myself earlier, but I didn't have a chance to do so. I just assumed you knew who I was. I am sorry. My client, Mr. Lee, can speak English very well, and we don't need an interpreter for his case."

Throughout the entire hearing, I could not help thinking the judge had probably never before met an Asian lawyer, in his chamber at least. Perhaps an occasional Asian person in his chamber was either a criminal defendant (if he was bad) or an interpreter (if he was good).

The prosecutor sought ninety days of jail time for Mr. Lee. I negotiated very hard, and we eventually agreed to only thirty days. I felt very good about the result. But as soon as I realized that Mr. Lee was a divorced man, with no family members to visit him, I suddenly felt a strong surge of sympathy for him. My brief moment of feeling out of place in the courtroom would be nothing compared to Mr. Lee's thirty days of isolation and incarceration, during which his only friends would be loneliness and a Korean-language Bible I gave him.

Over the next ten years, the courts in Minnesota have become much more diverse. In the metro counties, there are many judges, prosecutors, and lawyers of color, and there are efforts to achieve diversity in suburban and rural district courts, as well. Diversity in the courtroom is good because without it, those administering justice cannot fully understand other people's backgrounds and circumstances.

After appearing in criminal cases for years wearing my regular suit and a tie, I discovered the secret of distinguishing myself from felons and interpreters: wear a bow tie. When I wear a colorful bow tie, usually the judges assume I am a lawyer rather than a felon. Since I began to appear in the courtroom wearing a bow tie, nobody has mistaken me for a felon. So far so good.

I met a judge who also shared a similar experience of diversity in the courtroom. Recently I attended a bar association's annual gala, and I met the Honorable Donovan W. Frank, a federal district court judge, who has two adopted Korean daughters. I shared with Judge Frank my experience in Minnesota courtrooms at an early stage of my legal career. Surprisingly, he told me that, throughout his career as a judge for several decades, he saw judges and lawyers who were truly surprised to encounter people of color who became lawyers. He told me that kind of inexperienced viewpoint is not limited to the state courts; it is seen in the federal court system, as well. "We definitely should introduce more education on diversity within the legal circles," he said. With a smile on his face, Judge Frank continued, "In the meantime, Counsel, I think it is a good idea to wear a colorful bow tie in the courtroom, so you are not mistaken as a felon!"

Irish + Nepalese = Success

> The ultimate measure of a man is not where he stands in
> moments of comfort and convenience, but where he stands
> at times of challenge and controversy.
>
> —Martin Luther King, Jr.

Not many lawyers regard their clients as their best friends. But there
are a few instances when clients and attorneys become almost like a
family, after spending so many years together and witnessing each
other's ups and downs. My relationship with Valerie and Mike is one
such example. This Irish-American couple started their business in
the basement of their house in Saint Paul. Mike had a computer
software and fine art background, and Valerie was a teacher. As
soon as their children were grown and independent, they decided
to start their own web design business. After achieving moderate
success in a few years, they moved the business from their basement
to a small office building. With more space and new business coming
in steadily, they decided to hire some employees. One of their first
employees happened to know me, so I became the company's lawyer.
That was about fourteen years ago.

Their company became one of the biggest and most successful

in the industry of website design and development, with some Fortune 500 companies on its client list. Mike, the CEO, is usually in charge of new business development or rainmaking. Valerie, the CFO and secretary, is in charge of everything internal. Valerie listens to everyone's problems, both professional and personal, and I think she is one of the key reasons why this company became so successful. As I recall, this couple has occasionally offered their employees the opportunity to go to graduate school at the company's expense. They believe that this kind of offer results in a win-win situation for both the employer and employee. I am not very familiar with theories of corporate growth; however, I think Mike and Valerie's generosity toward their employees played a major role in their company's continued success and growth, year after year.

Sometimes they also encountered unexpected bumps in the road, but with remarkable resilience and courage, they always overcame the obstacles. One year, Val was diagnosed with cancer, but with early detection, strong faith, and plenty of support from family and friends, she overcame it. I visited her soon after she had surgery. Valerie's recovery from cancer meant a lot for me personally because my elder sister in Korea also had similar surgery around the same time, and I felt terribly guilty for not being able to visit her at one of the most difficult times of her life. When I saw Val at her office after the successful surgery, it was as if I saw my own sister in Korea, who was recovering from her own surgery. I gave Valerie a big hug, as if I were holding my own sister, and I tried to hide my tears from her. If Valerie saw my tears, she would have wondered why I was crying about her recovery.

In the past ten years or so, Mike and Valerie have hired as many as thirty plus Asian employees with a computer science background. I have worked on their immigration petitions and provided consultation on labor law, various compliance issues, and tax law issues, as well.

What puzzled me most was the presence of Nepalese employees at this company, which I don't see often in my other client companies. When I have told my lawyer friends in town that I developed a large number of clients who are IT professionals from Nepal, many simply refused to believe me. One friend said, half-jokingly, "Nepalese IT specialists? I never heard of such a thing. Isn't the entire nation composed of Buddhist monks, chanting and always bowing? How can they possibly be in the IT industry?" Another friend said, "Aren't they usually asylum seekers in the United States?"

Well, here is a story that may enlighten my friends who didn't believe me. Years ago, Minnesota State University, located in a small city called Mankato, Minnesota, about one hour's drive to the south of the Twin Cities, initiated a bold attempt to diversify its student body. The leaders of the university decided to recruit more students from Asia. Unlike other colleges and universities that were recruiting Asian students from large or more established countries, such as China, Japan, or Korea, the Mankato school decided to seek students from underdog countries, such as India, Bangladesh, Nepal, Turkey, and Pakistan. To make sure that this bold plan would work, Mankato also offered scholarships and reduced tuition options to the students coming from these countries. The result was a great success. Every year, three hundred to four hundred students came from these countries, enriching the student body. In recent years, as many as 150 Nepalese students have studied at Minnesota State University annually.

I don't exactly know how and why Valerie and Mike began hiring these Nepalese graduates, but this combination of Irish employers and Nepalese employees turned out to be almost like putting fish in water. From the very beginning, these Nepalese workers were highly disciplined, diligent, and hardworking, and all they needed was a gentle nudge from an encouraging employer.

It was a pleasure and honor on my part to see these young Nepalese IT specialists grow both professionally and personally. Sometimes I played the role of their friend or brother as well as their attorney.

One special occasion in the lives of two young Nepalese citizens is particularly vivid in my memory. Sudeep, a young computer engineer, and Priyanka, a charming lady living in Minneapolis, decided to marry each other. Usually, it is none of my business when my clients get married, but when I heard they could not bring their family members and friends from Nepal to Minnesota to celebrate their wedding, I felt genuinely sorry and decided to do something about it. I thought of inviting them to my house, but our family is only four people, and that wouldn't be festive enough. I lamented that I didn't have the power to convene one hundred people with just one day's notice. . . . But all of a sudden, a crazy idea came to me. There are plenty of good people at Edina Rotary Club, and I thought they may listen to my plea. So I asked Edina Rotary Club members to become wedding guests and witnesses for this couple.

I invited Sudeep and Priyanka to come to an Edina Rotary Club meeting. When they showed up, I introduced them to the staff members of Edina Country Club. The staff all understood the situation of the young couple from Nepal, and they arranged a special cake to celebrate their union. More than one hundred members of the Rotary Club of Edina gave their blessings to this couple. About one month later, Sudeep and Priyanka took me out to dinner, and they told me that, in honor of the totally unexpected blessing from Edina Rotary Club, they decided to keep the cake, which was made by the staff of the Edina Country Club, in their freezer as long as they lived in Minnesota. When I conveyed this story to the staff members of the country club, they were overjoyed.

As for Valerie and Mike's business, when the young employees began to start a family, it became more and more difficult for young mothers to balance between work and baby rearing. Valerie had a similar dilemma when she was young, and she decided to implement a day care within the company. As soon as the day care was added to the office, young employees who recently became parents could continue to work. I thought it was a fantastic idea.

Mike once told me that he never forgets the story he heard from his grandfather. It was extremely difficult for his grandfather to leave famine-stricken Ireland and come to settle in the United

States. His grandfather had no money whatsoever when he began his new life in this new continent. He married a girl who was an orphan from Chicago, and the young couple eventually settled in a small town called Hutchinson, Minnesota. In honor of his humble ancestors, Mike always tried to live frugally and faithfully. As soon as Mike made enough money from his computer business, he re-purchased his grandmother's house and land in Hutchinson. A couple of years ago, I was invited to the barn that Mike and Valerie rebuilt with their diligent work every weekend. As Mike showed me around, I was impressed by the museum-like quality of the barn, where Mike's grandparents and parents used to live, work, and raise children and farm animals.

Most recently, Mike and Valerie started a winery business in Hutchinson, and it became very successful. This past summer, they harvested about eight hundred bottles of red wine, which is used in their computer business's annual open house to celebrate life, family, and business success.

I was once also invited to a business meeting where Mike and Valerie invited all their Asian employees, as well. I was impressed by the growth of their office, which is now about one hundred times bigger than their original office ten years ago. Mike said, "I am an immigrant's descendant, myself. My grandfather came from famine-stricken Ireland. He came to Pennsylvania and took the train to Chicago and eventually settled in Minnesota. Life for my ancestors was not easy, but somehow they made it. You know what? I still see the same saga of immigrants being written in this country—this time, not by the Irish but by the Nepalese. For me, Irish and Nepalese don't make any difference. Eventually our business will find its customers in Dublin or Katmandu. Who knows?"

When I heard Mike talking about Katmandu, I thought he was a very considerate CEO, embracing every employee in his business. As I drove back to my office from that meeting, I realized that, among all my clients, Mike's company was one of the few that didn't lay off any employees during the economic downturn since 2008. This company's remarkable accomplishment came as a result of Mike's extraordinary leadership, Valerie's exceptional care of all their employees, and the hard work of all the employees, which include Nepalese IT warriors.

There is a company in Minnesota where a bunch of young professionals from Nepal, who were all trained at Minnesota State University in Mankato, are growing together under the leadership of an Irish-American couple. The CEO is like their father, and the CFO is like their mother. These young IT specialists from Nepal have already changed the way many American companies conduct their business. Together, they will eventually reach customers around the world, including those in cities like Dublin or Katmandu. I am looking forward to that day.

Russian Astronaut's Pencil

In a thousand years, archaeologists will dig up tanning beds and think we fried people as punishment.

—Olivia Wilde

"Out of twenty-five girls in our class, twenty-two girls already have one," Maria defiantly declared.

"In my class, everyone has one. It's embarrassing not to have one," Nina complained.

"Wooj, I think it will be good if our daughters can communicate with us in emergency situations. They should have one," Jennifer reasoned.

Several years ago, we had this conversation daily. So I purchased cell phones for our two daughters, not realizing that this small gadget would change our (yes, our, not just our daughters') lives entirely.

The biggest change that came after our daughters got cell phones was visibly less communication from them (how ironic, considering the primary function of telephones!). As they began to communicate with their friends using cell phones, we, as a family, began to have much less communication among us. Even between the two of them, our daughters began to communicate through cell phones, usually by text messages to each other. Out of curiosity, I once looked at their texts on their cell phones while they were at home. Something like the following was on their screens:

Maria: Mom says dinner is ready.
Nina: Tell her I'll be down in 3 minutes.
Maria: She says NOW.
Nina: Just tell her I'll be down in 2 minutes.
Maria: She says NOW.
Nina: OK. OK. Geez . . .

I thought this was just a unique situation to our household, but I read an article in which I discovered that this apparently is a global phenomenon. According to a recent survey by the marketing firm Harris Interactive, nearly half of teens in the United States say their social lives would end without their cell phones, and nearly 60 percent credit their mobile devices for improving their lives. About 80 percent of teenagers in America today carry wireless devices. This truly is a wireless generation.

The impact of the cell phone on the life of an American teen is amazing. Judging from the way our two daughters treat their cell phones, I can tell that they view them as the key to their social lives. According to our daughters, a person's cell phone tells a lot about the owner's social status, popularity, hobby, as well as her personality and studiousness. Maria said her cell phone is now more important than her UGGs (Australian sheepskin boots), which used to be her number one asset until her cell phone was introduced into her life.

Our daughters told us that texting is better than talking because it provides certain advantages, such as multitasking, speed, and most importantly, the option to avoid unnecessary or cumbersome verbal communication. I admit also that texting could be fun when you have nothing else to do. With literally billions of text messages sent each day, it is no surprise that many teens today can text blindfolded!

Teens today seem all excited about the wide blue ocean known as the wireless world. The possibilities of future mobile devices look endless—we already have smart phones, smart TVs, MP3 players, GPS, Wi-Fi computers, and Wii (video game console)—and I am genuinely happy knowing that our daughters will enjoy this new world of technology.

We tried to convince our daughters it would be better for our family if we spoke to each other using our voices, instead of texting to call each other to dinner, but they said they need to save their energy for other "important" multitasking. When I asked them what other important tasks needed their energy, they gave me the following list: updating information on Facebook; following Twitter; keeping in touch with their friends via email and text messages; downloading music from iTunes and building their digital music library; keeping an eye on new cell phone models; downloading attractive ring tones on their cell phones; and finishing their homework by visiting certain websites designated by their teachers. As a man who grew up with none of these computer-related activities, I have an extremely difficult time understanding their world today. But for our daughters, cell phones seem to have become their body part or second nature, or a combination of both.

A few years ago, when our daughters went to a summer camp, the wise organizers of the camp came up with a policy of banning the use of cell phones throughout the entire two-week period. Even though our daughters admitted that this camp was one of the best experiences of their lives, they complained that this was also one of the most difficult times in their lives because they became anxious thinking about what was accumulating in their email accounts, Facebook, and text messages. As soon as the camp was over, they frantically began checking all these electronic accounts to see what had accumulated for two weeks. They were reading them as if they contained the keys to the vaults of heaven or something. When I saw them lost in their cell phones, I realized how addicted they became to today's wireless technology.

Does the advent of the wireless age make our children smarter?

The answer to this question seems to be negative. It does not! According to *The Wall Street Journal*'s January 4, 2013, article, "Students Fall Flat in Vocabulary Test," the average American high school student's vocabulary is about 18,000 words today, which is in stark contrast to 25,000 words about ten years ago. Apparently, the number dwindles every year. Alarmed by this survey, and in an attempt to make up for the lost opportunity to learn new vocabulary in an old-fashioned way because of the wireless age, I began to subscribe to magazines and newspapers for our daughters. I encouraged our daughters to read newspapers to increase their vocabulary and also to learn about the "analogue" world. They showed interest for a brief period of time, but soon they went back to their laptop computers and cell phones. Then one day, at the end of a discussion as to how I can help them read newspapers, Nina made a suggestion that I purchase an iPad for her. If I purchased this electronic gadget, then she would read more newspapers and books, wherever she may go and whenever she wants. Maria said I didn't have to bother, because she can get the newspaper articles on her smart phone anyway.

Nina claimed that there are plenty of reasons why we should choose electronic versions of newspapers as opposed to paper versions. According to her, we cut more than 125 million trees every year to print books and newspapers, and unless we find a more eco-friendly and viable alternative, the deforestation will bring a devastating result for generations to come. (I discovered that this number is fairly accurate. Wikipedia confirms that as many as 500,000 trees are cut down to make each week's Sunday newspapers all over the United States.) When I went to purchase another gadget, called an iPad, I realized that the new wireless age found full expression in literally hundreds of new products. I felt I was definitely falling behind the accelerated advancement of technology.

Since then, I developed a habit of visiting the computer store near my office on a weekly basis, just to familiarize myself with products such as iPod, iPad, tablets, Kindle, MP3, MP4, and other gadgets, but each time I went, somehow I came to a conclusion that a simple newspaper I can actually hold in my hand and a radio I can actually turn on and turn off with my fingers are just sufficient enough for me to keep in touch with the world.

When I was our second daughter's age, I lived in a small house in Busan, Korea. In addition to our own family, my father's three siblings (one uncle and two aunts) lived with us. At one point, nine people lived in a four-bedroom house, and to this day, I just wonder how we managed to live together. In this nine-person family, our only source of information was the morning newspaper, which we always placed in our bathroom so that one person could read it in a most leisurely manner. Since we didn't have the kind of toilet paper we use today, out of necessity, we used the same newspaper to clean our behinds, too. In this moment of necessity, usually we sacrificed the international section first, thinking that it had the least amount of impact on our rather simple and parochial daily lives. Then the pecking order was politics, business, sports, travel, and classified ads.

Over breakfast and dinner, which we always had together, we had a chance to communicate with all the family members about what we learned in the bathroom by reading the same newspaper. My father always had the most information because he was always the first person to bring the paper to the bathroom, and he was the only person who had a chance to read the entire paper. I was usually at the bottom of the totem pole and could read only what my other family members left, so I had to listen to my parents and my elder sister for the sections I didn't get to read.

I remember reading a lot of travel sections (usually that was the only section left for me), but it was not so bad because I became the expert on other countries and cultures in our family. When my uncle lost his job and was looking for a new employment, we decided not to use the classified ads section to clean our behinds, for his sake. After he found another job, we resumed cleaning our behinds with classified ads section. When we washed our hands, we used an extra amount of soap because the ink from the newspaper was not easy to remove. Sometimes I could tell at our school who went number two before coming to class from the newspaper ink on their hands. Usually the more ink the kids had on their hands, the smarter they were.

I admire the new technology. Even today people can certainly bring an iPad or tablet or Kindle to the bathroom and get the same amount of information, which will not diminish in any way for the next family member, unlike the old-fashioned newspaper. In a way, digital gadgets are democratic and convenient for everyone. But nobody will read it as intensely as I did forty years ago in Korea, when, unless I read and memorized it, it would go down the toilet by the end of the day. Back then, in two or three days, all the information we could read went down the toilet, and, therefore, we all appreciated the tangible newspaper much more than we do today. And I believe the transitory nature of our only source of information made our life more precious and interesting.

At school, if someone said Elizabeth Taylor starred in *Gone with the Wind*, or the next Olympic Games will be held in Austria as opposed to Australia, or American students do not go to school on Mondays, for lack of better or other written sources, we just believed it, and our lives didn't change a bit for better or for worse. Anyone could say, "I saw it in the newspaper," and we just had to believe him, because, the chances were, the priceless source already went down the toilet anyway, and there was no way to verify the contested information. It may sound a bit like dark ages for young children today, but for some mysterious reason, I feel a deep nostalgia about those days.

I am sure gadgets, such as the iPad or Kindle, are useful. But I don't think I will appreciate them as much as the tangible newspaper, which I can turn, fold, smell, tear, and cut. In addition, where can I find such a luxury to kill a fly or mosquito or spider with or use to clean my behind, if necessary?

When I was ten, I was an expert on Turkey and Finland because I was the only one who read the travel section on a daily basis. And I had a chance to boastfully talk about these countries at school or over dinner to impress my friends or family members, who in turn told me what they read in the newspaper. I miss those days.

I read the following story on the Internet. According to *The Printed Owl* (September 8, 2010), during the initial space flights, NASA discovered that ordinary pens didn't work under zero gravity conditions. To solve the problem, NASA formed a committee and spent six years and two million dollars designing a pen for use in space. The pen would finally work under zero gravity conditions because of the pressurized ink inside, and it would work under sub-zero weather conditions, underwater, on glass, and on virtually any surface known to man. Feeling proud about their achievement, NASA researchers asked their Russian counterparts how they solved the same problem. Apparently, it didn't take even one day for Russian scientists to figure it out. They came up with a pencil, which didn't cost two million dollars or need a committee of scientists. When I shared this story with our daughters, they just laughed. I hope that one day they learn that the simple, old-fashioned way of doing things is sometimes better than the modern, high-tech way.

Sometimes we need to go back to basics. Starbucks came up with a new drink in honor of its fortieth anniversary. It is sugar-free, fat-free, and whipped cream-free, too. Can anyone guess this new product's name? Yes, it is called coffee. It took forty years for this coffee giant to go back to basics. I am sure our two daughters will call me old for saying this, but I want a coffee mug to have only coffee in it, nothing else. If I could have a newspaper and a pencil with an eraser attached to it to play a crossword puzzle (I like to erase my mistakes) and a phone nearby, in case I need to call someone (either from the wall or wireless), my Sunday morning will be good enough. If I may add a simple coffee with sugar to this list, I will be the happiest man in the world.

Today I like basic things. My daughters say I am getting old. Maybe. But I would like to tell my daughters: eventually, you will reach a point in life when a cup of coffee should contain coffee in it, and nothing else.

Life after Fifty

A rabbi once approached a member of his congregation and said, "Whenever I see you, you are always in a hurry. Tell me, where are you running all the time?" The man said, "I am running after success; I am running after fulfillment; I am running after reward for all my hard work." The rabbi responded, "That's a good answer if you assume that all those blessings are somewhere ahead of you, trying to elude you, and if you run fast enough, you may catch up with them. But isn't it possible that those blessings are behind you, that they are looking for you, and the more you run, the harder you make it for them to find you?"
—Harold Kushner, *When All You've Ever Wanted Isn't Enough*

Jennifer told me there would be a post-election party at Arneson Acres Park on November 10, where some neighbors, friends, and elected officers would celebrate the result of the 2012 election. When she began to purchase a lot of food, I thought it was a bit odd. What is there to celebrate after the election? Did the election change our lives much? Was Jennifer successful in electing the people she wanted? On the morning of November 10, Jennifer said she needed to go to the park early because she was on the party planning committee. After she and our two daughters left to prepare for the party, I decided to clean our guest room for our Rotary exchange student, who would be staying with us for the next three months.

My younger sister, Jiwon, a visiting scholar from South Korea at the University of Minnesota, came to have dinner with me.

After dinner, my sister and I headed to Arneson Park pavilion to join the neighbors and local elected officers, including our city's mayor and legislators. As soon as we entered the building, however, I heard a thundering "Surprise!" from everyone in the building. I am not a political candidate seeking any office, nor could I think of any reason why anyone would surprise me. But as soon as I saw the sign "50" all over the room, I realized that it was a surprise birthday party for me.

I was surprised that there were more than eighty people who gathered to celebrate my birthday. I gave each of them a big hug. I saw some I hadn't seen for more than a decade.

Our younger daughter, Maria, read a short and sweet poem that she had written, then our older daughter, Nina, showed a video clip of pictures with background music to show some major events in my life, and then Jennifer read a touching but also humorous poem she had written about our life together so far. Finally they gave me a chance to speak.

"Thank you, everyone! I am speechless. I expected to meet the mayor and other politicians, but none of them are here. You definitely surprised me. However, I must tell you something that may come as a surprise to you. You may have been tricked by Jennifer. Today is not my birthday. Even though my driver's license says my birthday is November 5, that is not my birthday, either. I was not born on November 5; I was born on March 19, 1962. When I was born, the infant mortality rate was very high in Korea, and virtually every child had to wait at least one hundred days before the birth was registered with the county office.

"When I was born, more than 90 percent of babies were born at home, instead of a hospital or clinic. I was born at my grandparents' house, which was in a remote countryside. My grandparents decided to wait at least one hundred days to see whether I would survive. Being a busy farmer, my grandfather somehow forgot to report my birth for eight months. He didn't have a car, and he had to walk more than four hours to get to the nearest county office in order to report my birth. When he arrived at the county office, he realized that there was a small fine assessed as penalty for those who didn't report the childbirth within one hundred days of the birth. A bit scared, and also not having any money with him to pay the fine anyway, he had the following conversation with the county clerk:

> County Clerk: What brought you here, old man?
> Grandpa: To report my grandson's birth.
> County Clerk: When was he born?
> Grandpa: Yesterday.

"So my legal birthday became November 5 instead of March 19. Ever since, throughout my entire life, I rarely celebrated my birthday. It was just confusing and cumbersome to have to remember two birthdays. But tonight, I finally accept the fact that I have two birthdays, and also that I am turning fifty, regardless of my true birthday!

"I was born to one of the poorest families in one of the poorest countries in the world. Our family had very little money, and the only way I could realize my dream of studying overseas was by getting a scholarship. Were it not for the Rotary Ambassadorial Scholarship, I don't think I would be celebrating my fiftieth birthday with all of you in this room. I received $23,800 in 1990 to come to study at the University of Minnesota Law School. I know that money would be worth more than two million dollars today, if properly invested. I often wonder whether I am worth a two million-dollar return to those Rotarians who invested in me by giving the scholarship. I served as the president of the Rotary Club of Edina this past year, in an attempt to pay back to Rotary. My family decided to host an international exchange student for the next three months. This is also my way of paying back to Rotary what I owe. I have been paying back to Rotary, but I still feel I carry a Rotary scholarship mortgage of more than two million on my shoulders."

Everyone seemed to enjoy my story and one friend said, "Why don't you celebrate both birthdays from now on? The first fifty years of your life, you said you didn't celebrate much. You should celebrate twice every year for the next fifty years to offset the first fifty years." We all laughed.

My grandfather, who created this mess, passed away at the age of fifty-six when I was only nine years old. He had a stroke, and died within two years. Scientists predict that we human beings will soon live beyond one hundred years. If their prediction becomes a reality, then I should get ready to celebrate another fifty birthdays. If not every year, I am thinking these days that perhaps I should celebrate my birthday once every other year. It was fun to celebrate my birthday with so many friends, even though it was not my real birthday. I am sure my grandfather wished me success and longevity when I was born, and little did he know that he caused my birthday to turn into a conversation piece. Grandpa, I miss you, and I thank you for giving me two birthdays!

At this surprise birthday party in November 2012, more than fifty friends came to celebrate my fiftieth birthday. (Photo Credit: John Flynn)

Rotary and Me

Clearly, we are moving toward a future that will be characterized at once by desperate needs and vast potential. We Rotarians are especially well positioned to serve as a bridge between the problems and the possibilities. We have a strong presence in nations that are technology-rich as well as in countries that can barely meet even the most basic human needs. Let us use that presence—and the unique perspective it affords us—to create the vibrant spirit of Rotary . . . and extend it to every part of the globe.

—Carlo Ravizza, quoted in *The Rotarian*, July 1999

Rotary Is Enough Guarantee to Trust You

No person was ever honored for what he received. Honor
has been the reward for what he gave.

—Calvin Coolidge

Recently I took an old man to a French restaurant. In fact, I
meant to have this lunch with him for the past eighteen years, but
somehow we never found a mutually agreeable time. He came to my
office, we exchanged pleasantries, and I took him to the restaurant.
I thanked him for lending me a significant amount of money when
I urgently needed it. To my surprise, he thanked me for giving him
the opportunity to serve me.

Over lunch I said, "Thank you, Gary, for trusting me." I wanted
to thank him for helping me eighteen years ago by gladly taking
the job of publishing my two books with no guarantee of payment
from me, a fresh law school graduate.

Gary said very slowly, "Wooj, you are most welcome. Actually,
I did not trust you, to be quite frank. Instead, I trusted Rotary.
Since you were once a Rotary Ambassadorial Scholar, I somehow
forced myself into trusting you. I knew that you would pay me
back because our relationship originated from Rotary, and I was

right. Maybe I should thank you for trusting me with publishing your books. Thanks for remembering me, and this lunch, too."

I told him, "I meant to buy this lunch eighteen years ago, but life has been too busy for both of us."

To which Gary said, "I understand. We both helped the recent immigrants from Korea by publishing those two books. I feel proud of your books, and I am honored to know that I was the publisher."

So, this is a story about a man, named Gary Brahms, whom I met about two decades ago—a man who trusted me and decided to publish my books, with no guarantee.

*　　*　　*

During law school, many Koreans living in the United States contacted me. Sometimes several Korean churches in Minnesota contacted me because they needed representation for various legal problems. On one occasion, I helped a church apply for a nonprofit status so it could become tax exempt. As I was still a law student, I had to get special permission from the court to appear before the judge on some cases. Occasionally I also helped people who were involved in criminal or family law matters, such as divorce or child custody. Sometimes I was called by the court to provide translation or interpretation services.

One day when I was in my second year of law school, David Jensen, a lawyer in Anoka County in Minnesota, and Reverend Jin Baik called and asked me to help with a criminal case. Two Korean brothers were being prosecuted in Anoka for purchasing half a dozen bear gall bladders, which some Koreans believe have special medicinal value for people with incurable diseases, such as cancer. The brothers' argument was that they purchased the gall bladders to give to their mother, who had suffered from cancer for a long time. The brothers and their mother were Korean immigrants living in Chicago. The brothers had come to Minnesota as migratory contractors in search of construction work. I was curious as to how the judge would solve the problem, and I was quite impressed by the judge's thoroughness as the case was presented to him. The judge actually called the doctor at the hospital in Chicago where the mother was being treated. The judge discovered that, apparently, the two brothers were telling the truth about their mother's cancer. After hearing the arguments from both sides (the brothers and the prosecutor), the judge said the brothers' intent was good when they purchased the gall bladders for their ill mother; however, they were still in violation of Minnesota's criminal code, which bans the trade of illegal animal body parts. Feeling sympathetic toward the two defendants' efforts to save their mother's life, the judge eventually ordered them to be released on the condition that they pay a small fine. The brothers were extremely happy to be free after a speedy trial, which meant they didn't have to waste any valuable workdays. I was glad the judge gave me an opportunity to function as a cultural interpreter between the Korean defendants and the court system in Minnesota. The brothers finished their contract work in Minnesota and, as soon as they got back to Chicago, they sent me a letter to thank me for believing in their innocence and their faith in the medicinal power of bear gall bladders.

After a series of incidents like this, I discovered that many Korean immigrants in the United States were not knowledgeable enough about the American justice system. So I began to summarize, in the Korean language, the basic principles of US law, such as criminal law, family law (wills, divorce, child custody, alimony, property division), immigration law, bankruptcy, and insurance, among other subjects.

I embarked on this book project during my second and third year of law school, but I didn't finish the first draft of the book until after graduation. In early 1994, I finished this project and passed the bar exam at the same time. When I finished my manuscript, it was about two hundred pages long. I made frequent trips to Kinko's to make copies, just in case people needed them. I believe I spent about two hundred dollars to make about one hundred photocopies, initially. My plan worked out very well at the beginning. Every time I met any Korean person who needed a simple answer to a legal problem, instead of taking it as a new case and charging one hundred dollars per hour, I just sent a five-dollar booklet to the client. This booklet was titled: *How to Solve Your Legal Problem in the United States Without Paying $5,000 to a Lawyer.* I think the photocopied book sold well, not because it was a great book, but because the title caught people's attention.

Soon my phones (both home and office) were flooded with calls from Koreans around the country, all looking for a copy of my book. Until then I didn't know there were so many Koreans in the United States. I made photocopies of my book almost every day to meet the demand of Koreans who wanted to get a copy. When I could not deal with the increasing demand any more, I discussed my dilemma with my godfather, Bill Clynes.

Bill is an engineer. He likes to solve problems. He introduced me to Milt "Beaver" Adams. Milt is a businessperson. He also likes to solve problems. Milt was working as a sales agent for several publishing companies. He thought Burgess International Publishing Company in Edina, Minnesota, would be good for me and introduced me to Gary Brahms, the CEO of Burgess International.

As CEO of a substantial publishing company, Gary was a busy man. As we met each other, Gary had just one concern, and it was well justified. His concern was whether this book would sell and make money. To convince him, I showed him my original manuscript and a photocopy, which had been selling well.

Gary said, "So, gentlemen, you want me to publish this book. Let me take a closer look."

Noticing that Gary was holding my manuscript upside down, I tried not to laugh. I said, "Well, Mr. Brahms, I know you would not be able to read it much because it is written in the Korean language. Basically, it is written to help Korean immigrants living in the United States understand US law. Let me point out that this is the first book of its kind, and I am 100 percent confident that more than two million Koreans living in cities, such as Los Angeles, Chicago, and New York, will buy a copy. The copies I made from Kinko's have been selling well. The book will do well."

"How about the Twin Cites?" Gary wanted to know whether I would sell the books in the local market, as well.

"There are about ten thousand Koreans living in the Twin Cities area, but I don't think I will target them as my primary market. Let me deal with bigger markets like Los Angeles, Chicago, and New York first, and then I will consider Minnesota."

"Okay, fair enough. How are you going to market the books? Do you have a plan?"

When I heard this question, I noticed that he developed some interest in my book, and I knew that I had very little to lose by being frank with him. I said, "I don't have any plans. But for some reason, people so far managed to find me, and they have been screaming for me to send them a copy. I have sent about two hundred photocopies in just one month. I bet the folks who bought and read my manuscript will all become my book's supporters. As soon as I have money in my account, I will place advertisements with all the major Korean language daily newspapers in big cities like Los Angeles, Chicago, and New York."

Realizing that I needed help, Milt Adams kicked in. "Gary, I know this is not the best business proposal, but I am so impressed with this young man's good intent. We should help him. This time alone, let's publish it and see what happens."

After twisting his eyebrow a few times with his fingers, Gary gently pushed my manuscript across the table to my side and said, "Wooj, I heard from Bill Clynes that you received a Rotary International Ambassadorial Scholarship to study at the University of Minnesota Law School. I am a Rotarian myself. Even though I cannot read your manuscript, I somehow feel that your book will sell and benefit many people. I will publish the first ten thousand copies at my expense. But promise to pay me back if you sell them and make money. If you don't make money, then let's regard it as a gift from both of us to the new immigrants from Korea."

What he said was overwhelming. I didn't notice that tears were streaming down my cheeks. As Gary wanted, the meeting ended within ten minutes. I profusely thanked them both and called Bill to thank him, as well, as soon as I came back to my office. I had to revise and rewrite a new preface to include and recognize these people's names. I forwarded a revised manuscript to Burgess International Publishing Company sometime in August 1994, and exactly ten thousand copies of my books were published and delivered to my office in less than one month. I was just glad I didn't have to go to Kinko's to produce time-consuming photocopies any more.

Originally I thought of just one book, but I decided to publish two separate books. The first one was titled *Basic Principles of US Law*, and the second book was titled *200 Questions and Answers to Help Koreans Understand US Law*. When these two books were published, I felt as if a pit in my stomach was removed. It was such an uplifting and refreshing feeling to see my books ready to meet their readers around the United States.

* * *

My office became half law practice and half warehouse for my books. Every time I looked at those boxes of books, however, an overwhelming feeling of heavy burden began to weigh on my shoulders, and it quickly eclipsed my initial feeling of pride, relief, and joy as an author, because, frankly, I didn't know how to sell them, nor did I have an immediate marketing plan or strategy for those books. I felt like a juvenile parent who didn't know how to take care of an unplanned or undisciplined child. People still called me and purchased one or two books a day. However, at that rate, it would take as many as fifteen years to sell all the books that were published already.

Sensing the mounting urgency of the situation, I scraped together every dollar I had and placed an advertisement in *The Korea Central Daily* in Chicago, but no one responded to the advertisement. I became desperate and terrified. I borrowed a few hundred dollars from my friends and relatives, and this time, I placed a full-page ad with the two largest Korean language papers—*The Korea Times* and *The Korea Central Daily*—in Los Angeles, where people said something like 1.5 million Koreans lived.

Soon thereafter, I had to drop this project when, one October morning, Jennifer said with a tone of urgency, "Wooj, my water just broke. I feel contractions." I drove Jennifer to the emergency room, and our first baby, Nina, was born on October 30, 1994. While I was with Jennifer and Nina at the hospital, I completely forgot about my office and books. When I went back to my office finally, I discovered that about 120 people had sent checks to buy my books. To this day, I believe that our daughter Nina was a miracle—not only because she was born, but because she brought good fortune to us.

When I realized I could not physically handle the increasing book orders any more, I decided to hire a person to process the incoming telephone and mail orders. I also launched a "1-800-xxx-WOOJ" toll-free phone number to promote sales, and also to answer any questions from the readers of my books.

To everyone's surprise, it took only a few months for me to pay back $15,000 to Gary Brahms, the CEO of Burgess International Publishing Company. I believe it was one snowy December or January day when I personally delivered the last check to him. As usual, Gary was busy, but this time he offered me a cup of tea, knowing that he wouldn't see me for a while after receiving the final check from me.

When his secretary brought the tea, Gary proudly introduced me to her again, even though I knew her already. "Hey, Kelly, this is the famous author, Wooj. He made our company rich with his books." I knew he was just joking, but I felt great when he said it. I thanked him again for believing in me. Gary said that my being a Rotary Ambassadorial Scholar was good enough surety for him to take the chance with my book idea, and that he didn't have to worry about the payment. He said it many times to me already, but it was a very humble moment for me every time I heard it from him.

When I stepped out of Gary's office, the snow blanketed the entire world. I vividly remember how beautiful the snow-covered world looked and how relieved I felt knowing that I just delivered the last check to the publishing company. Rotarians Bill Clynes, Milt Adams, and Gary Brahms all trusted me, even though I had nothing but dreams. They all trusted me just because I was once a recipient of the Rotary International Ambassadorial Scholarship!

I believe I reached approximately one hundred thousand Korean people with my books (I am assuming that one book would have been read by at least ten people, because many copies were sold to churches and libraries.) I can't remember how many telephone calls I received from those readers, but they all helped me by presenting more challenging and interesting legal questions.

In this whole process—from the concept to writing to editing to publishing and marketing—there were many bumpy roads where I was totally lost and almost gave up the entire project. Thankfully, many guardian angels, including Rotarians, came to my rescue and gave me sufficient encouragement and inspiration so that I could finish the task of enlightening the recent immigrants from Korea to the United States with my books.

I had a firm handshake with Mr. Paul Harris, who founded Rotary International over a century ago. I visited Rotary International's head office in Evanston, Illinois, in 2007.

Why Do People Join Rotary?

Man himself is a precarious balance between love and
hate, generosity and selfishness, peaceableness and
aggressiveness. He is not perfectible but he is improvable,
and nothing in his history or his nature obliges one to
abandon belief in him. He may indeed be forever "trapped
between Earth and a glimpse of heaven," but he will hold
to that glimpse, as we must.

—Eric Sevareid

What do the following people have in common: Winston Churchill,
Douglas MacArthur, George C. Marshall, Franklin D. Roosevelt,
Albert Schweitzer, J.C. Penney, Neil Armstrong, Gerald Ford, John
F. Kennedy, and Mother Teresa? Yes, they are heroes and they all
changed the world. But few people know they were Rotarians.
These heroes' legacies are inherited and continued by many other
Rotarians, who may be ordinary citizens, but who are still in
the business of turning the world into a better place for the next
generation.

Different people join different organizations for different
reasons. When I asked Rotarians why they joined Rotary, they gave

me a multitude of responses. Some joined Rotary because it was near where they lived or worked. Some joined out of obligation, whatever that obligation may be. Some people joined Rotary to broaden their professional horizons. Some joined because their parents were Rotarians. Some joined in their twenties; some joined after their spouses passed away; and some joined after retirement. Some wanted to reach out to people in other continents by joining Rotary. Regardless of the reasons they may have, Rotarians are all good folks, I concluded, because they believe in one goal: service above self.

In 2009, I received the following email from a member of our club, who forwarded a story originally written by Susan Strom, a Rotarian in Virginia, who received the Rotarian of the Year award from her club.

In her email, Susan mentioned "Camp Enterprise." This camp was established in 1980 by our own Edina Rotary Club and celebrated its thirtieth anniversary in 2010. Camp Enterprise provides an opportunity for high school seniors from Minnesota and Wisconsin to immerse themselves for three days in understanding the free enterprise system. Presentations are made by business executives and entrepreneurs, who share their experiences and answer questions on a variety of areas and interests. In just three days, these talented high school student campers usually come up with great business concepts, logos, marketing strategies, financing plans, and professional team building, all to the surprise of volunteering Rotarians. Rotarian volunteers then read their business plans, listen to their presentations, and grade them. On the last day of the camp, the best team receives a nominal million-dollar check, which is always a great honor for the receiving team and the high school they represent.

This is what Susan Strom wrote:

Why Did I Join Rotary?

On June 30, 2006, I had the honor of becoming my club's Rotarian of the Year in Manassas, Virginia. It was an honor that took me completely by surprise. My official membership in Rotary began in 2004, but my history with Rotary goes back much further.

As a high school senior in Wayzata, Minnesota, my civics teacher informed me that a local Rotary Club (Plymouth, Minnesota) was willing to sponsor a student to a three-day retreat called Camp Enterprise. She asked me if I'd be interested in attending and (to be honest) the thought of getting out of school sounded great!

The camp included students from throughout the Minneapolis suburbs—each sponsored by their local Rotary Club. These business professionals used their personal time to lead seminars in their various areas of expertise. They covered everything from how to obtain financing to investing in the stock market to business ethics. The topics and enthusiasm of the speakers enthralled me.

I still have my folder full of notes collected from those presentations. However, what remains most vivid in my mind is that the men and women who volunteered their time (and money) to sponsor me and teach me about business seemed to be having as much fun as I was as a participant. They genuinely cared about future generations and me as they shared their business experiences and encouraged us to think about the future. They were amazing examples of leadership and service.

In 2002, I incorporated and began my own marketing consulting company. Many of the concepts I have used to grow my business were first introduced to me at Rotary's Camp Enterprise.

Something special was ignited in me at Camp Enterprise as

I participated in those seminars. I saw that giving of one's time and energy to help others can make an impact that can resonate years later. Seeds were planted that continue to grow in me. I hope that I can encourage and reach out to others as much as those before me have. I am a Rotarian because, just like those before me, I want to work toward a better tomorrow. I've got big shoes to fill.

Unlike Ms. Strom, my encounter with Rotary came much later than high school when Rotarians in Busan, Korea, chose me as one of their final Ambassadorial Scholarship recipients to study overseas. That was when I was in my late twenties. Ever since I had that first encounter with Rotary, and after receiving the scholarship that made my dream real, I thought I should somehow return the favor. After spending the busiest three years of my life studying law in Minnesota, as soon as I began to make money, I thought it was time to begin paying back to Rotary so the circle would become full. In my case, the person who helped me most in becoming a Rotarian was Bill Clynes.

Bill Clynes was the first Rotarian I met in the United States in 1990, when he served as the coordinator for a dozen incoming scholars from overseas, including me. This rather quiet engineer has been a Rotarian for most of his life, and he has spent a lot of his own time and money hosting and helping international students. When I came to Minnesota, Bill spent a lot of time connecting students from Japan, Korea, the Philippines, Jamaica, Greece, and Sweden to Rotarian counselors in the Twin Cities area. Bill invited all these scholars to his house for major holidays, such as Thanksgiving, Easter, and Christmas. Through him, we all became very close friends among ourselves, too.

Every time we were invited to his house, Bill wanted to talk about his experience in Korea. Bill was based in Korea from 1948 through 1949 as a military engineer. He was only nineteen years old back then. Usually a tacit man, Bill always became excited whenever he spoke about Korea. After all, Korea was the only foreign country Bill spent a substantial amount of time in, and everything he lived through as a young man there was shocking enough for him to develop a long-lasting impression. In Korea, nineteen-year-old Bill saw poverty, disease, war, orphans, and nation building, and I strongly believe that this experience turned him into a humble and serving man for the rest of his life.

Bill and Lois are very humble people, but they know how to be generous with their time and money, particularly when it comes to helping international students. They may have only one biological son, but there are more than fifty-five former international students, who are now successful and established citizens all around the world and who call Bill and Lois their adopted parents in Minnesota. As far as I recall, these former scholars became a high-ranking government official in China, a director of engineering for an international hotel group in Greece, a dean at Duke University, a lawyer, several professors, and a TV personality in Japan, just to name a few.

The year I came to Minnesota, Bill connected me to a lawyer by the name of Dean Edstrom, who was also a fine Rotarian. While I was attending law school, I was cared for by many Rotarians, such as Bill and Dean. Between 1990 and 1991, in an attempt to do my duties as an ambassadorial scholar, I visited at least ten Rotary Clubs in Minnesota to deliver a speech about Korea. One winter day, I drove five hours (it took much longer than I expected because of the heavy snow) to visit Redwood Falls Rotary Club to deliver a speech that lasted only fifteen minutes. The president of that club owned a bed and breakfast business, and I spent one night there.

Each time I visited a different Rotary Club, I was warmly greeted and met equally good people who were all in the business of turning the world into a better place. After meeting so many wonderful people, I made up my mind that I should join Rotary.

There was another incident that made me decide to join Rotary. Years ago, I had a chance to see a Danish movie titled *Babette's Feast*, which was made in 1987. Here is a summary of the movie. In nineteenth century Denmark, two adult sisters lived in an isolated village where a French woman refugee, Babette, arrived at their door and begged them to take her in as a cook. After years of living with these two good-hearted Danish sisters, Babette won an unexpected fortune but asked the sisters to allow her to treat the entire village with her unexpected fortune. Although the two sisters and all the villagers were concerned about what Babette, a foreigner, might do with her unexpected fortune, the two sisters trusted and allowed her to prepare the meal. Babette then prepared the feast of a lifetime for the entire village. The sisters thought Babette didn't have to spend all her fortune to treat the villagers; however, Babette thought that it was her duty to pay them back.

When I saw this touching movie, somehow I thought that the two sisters and the people in that small village in Denmark were like the Rotarians I met in this country, who embraced and trusted me as one of their own. I thought it was my turn to pay back to the villagers as Babette did in the movie. Babette and I were both foreigners and beneficiaries of generous villagers across the ocean, and we were both guided by the people who were willing to lay the bridge for us to cross the troubled water in life. After watching this movie, I was convinced that I should join Rotary and try to pay back the benefit I received from it.

When I discussed my interest in paying back the amount of the scholarship, Bill Clynes said, "Wooj, the scholarship had its purpose, and the purpose was achieved when you used it. You successfully finished your studies and you became a lawyer. Rotary doesn't expect you to pay back. But I have an idea. If you still feel indebted to Rotary, why don't you join Rotary?" With this statement, he gladly sponsored me, and in 1995, I joined the Edina Morningside Rotary Club, which meets at seven o'clock every Tuesday morning. About two years later, when I realized I could not wake up early in the morning anymore, I switched to Edina Noon Rotary Club, which meets at noon every Thursday.

I am truly glad I joined Rotary. When I joined, I thought I would stay just until I paid back my scholarship, but interestingly enough, I kept receiving more benefits as I tried to pay back. Here are a few changes that occurred after I joined Rotary. First of all, as a former recipient of the scholarship myself, I am able to make a difference in other young people's lives by contributing to the Rotary International Scholarship fund, which enables young students today to go overseas to broaden their horizons. Secondly, I am able to continue friendships with many wonderful people, called Rotarians, who are all committed to service above self. And third, through Rotary, I am able to make a meaningful contribution to changing the world into a better place, on both a local and international level. For example, how could one person vaccinate all the children around the world against polio? It may have looked like an impossible project when it was launched; however, as a group, Rotary ended up wiping out 99 percent of polio around the world in the past twenty years. To this date, besides marrying my wife, Jennifer, I think joining Rotary was one of the best decisions I have ever made.

Recently, I found a very meaningful "definition of a Rotarian," which came from a former president of Bloomington Rotary Club in Minnesota. It goes like this:

A Rotarian is an Ordinary Person.

A Rotarian is an ordinary person who wants to do something extraordinary . . . to rise above the daily routine . . . to make a difference in a community and the world.

A Rotarian is an ordinary person who takes on a small task with unusual enthusiasm.

A Rotarian is an ordinary person who has a vision of the world at peace, brought about by goodwill and understanding.

A Rotarian is an ordinary person who sees three million children each year die from disease and asks: Why?

A Rotarian is an ordinary person who sees 1,200 Rotary Foundation Scholarships each year and asks: Why not more?

A Rotarian is an ordinary person who believes that truth is a difficult and worthy pursuit.

A Rotarian is an ordinary person who acts not out of convenience, but out of conviction.

A Rotarian is an ordinary person who believes that "service above self" is more than an ideal—it is a belief that transforms an ordinary person into an extraordinary member of the world community.

—James N. Lucas (president of Bloomington Rotary Club, 1987–1988)

I arranged for Bill Clynes, past president of Edina Rotary Club, to receive a Medal of Honor from the government of South Korea, for his service in Korea in 1947–1948. In this photo, Bill's son, David, is helping Bill's medal to be hooked properly. Two more Edina Rotary Club members (Harold Harris and Ron Erhardt) also received the same honor for their service in Korea more than sixty years ago.

Children and Rotary

Sow a thought, and you reap an act;
Sow an act, and you reap a habit;
Sow a habit, and you reap a character;
Sow a character, and you reap a destiny.

—Charles Reade

Rotary Club honors a member as a "Paul Harris Fellow" whenever he or she makes a donation of one thousand dollars to the Rotary International Foundation. Sometimes, Rotarians' family members make donations, as well, and they also receive the same recognition. When I witnessed Bill Clynes's (my godfather) family members—his wife, Lois, and his son, David—become Paul Harris Fellows, I thought I should encourage my own family members to become Paul Harris Fellows, too.

Ever since Nina (our first daughter) was a kindergartner, I occasionally brought her to our club's meetings. The first few times, she had no idea what Rotary was all about, but gradually she began to appreciate it, and one day, to my surprise, she told me she was impressed by Rotarians' willingness to serve and change the world. Sometimes I asked her to recite the definition of Rotary in front of our club members. Then she would say, "Rotary is a group of ladies and gentlemen who are committed to world peace and service for others." Our members enjoyed her a great deal every time she stood on her chair and recited her own definition of Rotary. I thought to myself that, for a young child, Nina may not understand such big concepts as world peace or service above self, but there will be a day when she becomes an adult and she will fully understand all these concepts.

At one meeting several years ago, Nina learned from our speaker of the week that there are children around the world who suffer from cancer, and who wear wigs during chemotherapy. I guess the speaker that week must have been extraordinarily inspirational because, at the end of the meeting, Nina decided to grow her hair so she could donate it to someone who needed a wig. After letting it grow for nearly five years, on June 14, 2008, Nina finally made the decision to cut and donate her hair. The hairstylist cut Nina's hair at no charge. When Nina came home with short hair, I thought I had the most beautiful child in the world. Maria, our second daughter, inspired by her elder sister, also wanted to do the same, and we allowed her to grow her hair to donate in the future, as well.

After hearing about the work of Rotaplast International, a nonprofit humanitarian organization providing free reconstructive surgery and treatment to those born with cleft palate and related anomalies in developing countries, Nina and Maria began to save money to help these unlucky children get surgery and regain the smile on their beautiful faces.

Edina Rotary Club members and family members deliver as many as 80 to 120 turkey baskets over Thanksgiving holiday every year. Nina and Maria have been involved in this project, as well, for the past ten years or so.

I strongly believe that bringing a child to Rotary Club meetings is one of the best investments a Rotarian can make for his/her child's future. Nina proved it to me by donating her hair to needy children, after being inspired by a speaker. I often tell our two daughters to consider joining Rotary when they become gainfully employed in the future. They usually smile, instead of giving me any definite answer, but I believe they will eventually become generous Rotarians, too.

This billboard photo became popular among Rotarians as it contained an important message: Not Your Father's Rotary. Rotary is becoming more diversified. (Photo Credit: Jennifer Bennerotte)

Purchasing a House, Rotary Style

We who lived in concentration camps can remember the men who walked through the huts comforting others, giving away their last piece of bread. They may have been few in number, but they offer sufficient proof that everything can be taken from a man but one thing: the last of human freedoms—to choose one's attitude in any given set of circumstances—to choose one's own way.

—Viktor E. Frankl

"Why can't we improve this room?" Jennifer complained to me.

"Yeah, why don't we?" our daughters joined in.

"Because I made a promise not to," was my simple response.

After buying our house, we modified it to the extent we wanted. However, there was one room we—or I, to be more precise—didn't change much. It remained in about the same condition as when we purchased it. Our two daughters blamed me for not "modernizing" the study up to the level of other rooms in the house. They began to spend a lot of time there doing their homework, and they felt the room was a bit too old-fashioned. Well, it may sound stupid or like a lazy man's lame excuse, but I had my own reason not to change it.

Here is a story about our study, on the door of which I recently put a sign reading "Mr. Kremer's Room."

To get closer to my office and to send our daughters to a better school district, we finally decided to move. We started the process of selling our old house, right in the middle of global economic recession and also the frozen real estate market. We hired an agent, who strongly encouraged us to contact an interior designer and an inspector prior to listing our house on the market. We knew that it would be an uphill battle, so we contacted these professionals to use their valuable services. We worked very hard to prepare our house for the market, but for the entire first month, only ten people came to see it. After forty-five days, we were nearly ready to lower the price, and then finally a serious inquiry came in. We said to ourselves: "Okay, if this person is not interested in our house, we will lower the price by at least ten thousand dollars." Two days passed without any response from this last interested person. As we prepared to lower the price, this last person made an offer. It was not the best offer, but we were just relieved to sell our house in one of the worst real estate markets in history.

As soon as we sold it, suddenly everyone wanted to sell their house to us. Not knowing what would be the best house for our future, we asked around and came to the conclusion that we should invest in a house that would appreciate the most while we lived in it. Some people gave us the advice that we could not go wrong by choosing a house near a golf course or with a lake view, which could easily increase the house's value significantly over time. After looking around at a dozen houses or so, we found a house that had a beautiful view of a golf course. The selling agent told us that this house had the potential of doubling our investment within the next few years. Perhaps because of his rosy prediction, we thought the golf course house was a great opportunity for us. We began to write an offer.

But then I received a call from Dick, a friend of mine from Edina Rotary Club. At one of our previous Rotary meetings, I happened to mention to Dick that I had sold my house in Burnsville and was looking for a house in Edina. Dick didn't say much at the time, but somehow he remembered to call me two days later and asked me to visit him. So Jennifer and I visited him.

Dick was a former politician. He served as a commissioner of Hennepin County (which is the largest of Minnesota's eighty-seven counties) for two terms in the 1970s and 1980s. Both he and his wife, Betty, had just turned eighty-five. Dick and I had known each other through Edina Rotary Club for the past eleven years.

Here is how I got to know Dick on a more personal basis. I believe it was in December 2002. I was talking to a client on the phone when my secretary informed me an old man had come to see me. She said he was holding a large photo frame. I thought a peddler had come to sell a painting or something, so I told my secretary to ask him to leave. But after ten minutes of talking on the phone with my client, I realized the peddler hadn't left. When I walked into my secretary's office, I was surprised to find Dick Kremer, who was holding a LARGE framed photo. I apologized for the long wait and asked him to enter my office, wondering what brought him to see me that day.

"Dick, why didn't you tell me it was you? I would have ended my phone conversation earlier." After a deep sigh, Dick said, "Oh, Wooj, that's quite all right. I am a retired man, and I have a lot of time on my side."

"So what brought you here?" I asked, not being able to detach my eyes from the large framed picture, which was about half my height.

"Well, my doctor says I have cancer now. Look here." He showed me a coin-sized spot on his head. It was very dark. "I was diagnosed with skin cancer. It may not kill me tomorrow, but it will kill me eventually. When I heard the news, at first I didn't know what to do, but then I decided to shed things I owned. I thought you might like to have this framed picture, so I brought it here. It is a picture of the new Hennepin County Government Center, which was built during my term as the county's commissioner."

Since I go to court hearings at Hennepin County Government

Center once in a while, I recognized the building's image immediately. But I was still wondering why he decided to give it to me. I said to him, "Dick, I am sorry to hear that you have cancer. I hope you recover soon. Regarding this picture, what an honor you chose me! But is there any reason why you chose me? You have six children, and there are more than 150 members at our Rotary Club. Why did you decide to give it to me?"

Dick looked around my office for a while, and then said, "Well, I know many lawyers. But you are the youngest lawyer I know. I am sure you go to the court once in a while, don't you? I thought you might like to hang this frame in your office because you're a lawyer who practices in the county. That's all. Well, I am tired. It's time for me take a nap, and I know I should let you go back to your business, young man. So long."

And he left. Just like that.

After that first visit in 2002, he came to my office at least three more times. The next time he came, he brought paintings by a famous Chinese artist, named Yang Yang, who once had a gallery of his own in a building in downtown Minneapolis, which Dick owned. When Yang couldn't pay the rent, he gave Dick his paintings instead, and Dick gave me three of Yang's pieces. Each time Dick came to my office, we discussed the progress of his cancer treatment. Dick said it was going well, and he was feeling much better since he began to shed things he owned.

Now, back to when I was busy writing an offer to purchase the house overlooking the golf course. Dick phoned and asked me to visit him. When Jennifer and I entered his house, both Dick and Betty were waiting for us. Dick said they had lived in their house for the past forty-nine years, during which he and Betty had raised their six children. He wanted us to buy his house.

After taking a sip of Coke, Dick said, "Wooj, I am old. You know I was diagnosed with cancer about five years ago. I probably didn't tell you this, but last year, I had a heart attack, too. I guess my health is not in the best condition. Now the only room I use in this house is our study on the main level. As for the other rooms, I cannot move around too much. Both Betty and I love this house a great deal, but we have decided to say goodbye to it. You see, a house becomes a burden when you reach certain age like mine. Betty and I discussed it a long time, and we decided to sell our house to someone we trust before we move to an assisted living facility. I know you are looking for a house, and we want to sell our house to you. You will honor us by purchasing this house from us."

Both Jennifer and I looked around the house. It was a bit old, but we liked it. It did not have a gorgeous view, but it was a very well built, dignified, and practical house on a quiet street. It was just the right size, and it had some recent upgrades to the kitchen and a beautiful sunroom, too.

We immediately withdrew our offer from the golf course house. Once we agreed to buy the house from Dick and Betty, we didn't have to talk much. At the end of a thirty-minute friendly talk, we shook hands to make a deal. As Rotarians usually do, all we had to do was apply a four-way test. Of all the things we think, say, or do, Rotarians always ask:

1. Is it the *TRUTH?*

2. Is it *FAIR* to all concerned?

3. Will it build *GOODWILL* and *BETTER FRIENDSHIPS?*

4. Will it be *BENEFICIAL* to all concerned?

As we applied this four-way test, there was no need to hire any agents between the two of us. We didn't have to negotiate much. Knowing his health situation very well, I told Dick to take as much time as he wanted before moving out of the house. We decided to split any outstanding bills in a most amicable way, on a fifty-fifty basis. I felt as if he were my father, and I am sure he regarded me as his son.

The only person I consulted about the purchase of this house was my father in Korea. When I explained how old Dick was, my father told me NOT to negotiate with him. He said, "Son, you buy his house. And you buy the house without negotiating. Obviously, this gentleman has a lot of emotional attachment to the house, and he seems to have a lot of pride in it, too. Don't ever hurt his feelings by trying to negotiate the price. Treat him like you treat me. You buy the house without giving him or his wife any trouble or headache. Remember, you are buying the house from him like you buy it from me. Never lose your respect for him throughout the entire process."

At the beginning, I didn't quite understand my father's advice, but gradually I began to see his wisdom. Psychiatrists tell us that moving is as stressful as losing a family member. My father was trying to tell me that it was unnecessary to create any extra stress for Dick or Betty in this transaction.

I candidly shared this cordial father-son discussion with Dick. Then Dick, with his eyes closed, said, "Even though I never met him, I like your father already. You told me that your parents went through the Second World War and Korean War. You see, your father and I have something in common. We know what poverty is like, and we know what war is like, too. We also know how to tighten our belts and rebuild the world around us. Your generation may be too young to understand all this, but your father and I certainly understand it. Even though we never met with each other, I feel as though I know your father already. I want you to invite your parents to your new house and introduce them to me, too."

With good advice coming from both my father and Dick at the same time, the transaction was as smooth as it could be and I felt just great. We had no reason to be in a hurry for the closing; however, the couple who bought our house needed to close within forty-five days because they were relocating from Chicago. This cop-nurse couple from Chicago had lined up jobs in the Twin Cities already and asked whether we could give them our furniture items, such as beds, dining room set, flat-panel TV, and stereo. When we heard this rather personal request, we were quite perplexed, but later we discovered they needed more furniture because they had five young children, ranging from one month to twelve years in age.

I discussed this request with my father, and my father's advice was simple: "Son, you told me he is a police officer. Be nice to a public servant. Give him whatever he wants!" So we decided to give this cop-nurse couple all the items they wanted.

We decided to vacate our house in a relatively short period of time, so we had to hurry to move into our new house. Fortunately, it took only a couple of weeks to seal the deal, but in the process, both Dick and Betty were extremely sad about saying goodbye to their house.

As we needed no negotiation, the only document necessary to finalize the deal was a simple purchase agreement. In it, I insisted we add the following provision:

> The buyer (Wooj) hereby agrees to leave the study in the house intact after moving in and agrees to make the room available and allow for the seller (Dick) to come to visit the room for a period of one year, at any time, with one day in-advance notice, so long as the seller uses the room for the purpose of reading or taking a nap.

When Dick saw this provision, he smiled. I somehow felt it was important to leave at least one room in the house in the same condition as when it was sold for Dick's honor and also for the sake of his memory of the house. So that's why I left our study in the same condition as when we purchased it. After we had moved in, I asked Dick a few times to visit our house to read or take a nap in the study. He just smiled instead of responding to my offer.

Dick Kremer passed away on July 26, 2010. I went to his funeral service, and in my eulogy of Dick, I shared the story of how I had purchased his house. Many people, including his six children and two dozen grandchildren, heard for the first time the details of how Dick sold his house to us. As I read the eulogy, I saw smiles on the faces of Dick's children and grandchildren, even though their eyes were filled with tears. Toward the end of the funeral service, I discovered that one of Dick's sons, John Kremer, was also a

Rotarian, which made me think that Dick left a big legacy in this world.

John Kremer and I became good friends. John recently traveled to South America on a Rotary-related mission. He is carrying the Rotary torch left by his father. I would like to invite him to our house one of these days and show the study where his father spent his life's last few years just to read a book or take a nap. I am sure he will like that visit.

Polio Eradication

A Splendid Torch:

I want to be thoroughly used up when I die,
for the harder I work, the more I live.
Life is no brief candle for me.
It is a sort of splendid torch which
I have got hold of for a moment,
and I want to make it burn as brightly
as possible before handing it on
to future generations.

—George Bernard Shaw

Every time I feel confused about life, I listen to the song "Both Sides Now," originally sung by Joni Mitchell, and later by Judy Collins, too. I discovered that these two famous folk singers had something in common: they were both stricken by polio when they were young. Remarkably, they both recovered from this horrendous disease and became successful singers.

Do you know anyone who has been stricken by polio? I have. One of my best friends in elementary school in Korea suffered from it. I remember occasionally carrying him on my back during our elementary school's third and fourth grade days, when we went on a school outing or when we had to climb the stairs. He was talented in many subjects and finished schools all the way through college, but after being rejected from job interviews, he became a hermit. We didn't hear from him for several years until one day when we heard that he committed suicide. We all lamented the loss of a friend who could have had a fulfilling life, were it not for polio. We thought what drove him to death was the society's prejudice, not polio itself. Perhaps he felt too powerless to single-handedly fight the discrimination and bias from society.

Since I joined Rotary, polio eradication has been one of Rotary International's most important ongoing projects. In some years, we set goals of individual member donations so that enough vaccine could be distributed among countries where polio is still crippling children. In 1988, the World Health Assembly (WHA), the annual meeting of the ministers of health of all member states of the World Health Organization (WHO), made a resolution to launch a global effort to eradicate polio. As a result of collective efforts made by the Global Polio Eradication Initiative (GPEI)—the single largest, internationally coordinated public health project mankind has ever known—by the end of 2006, only four countries remained polio-stricken: Nigeria, India, Pakistan, and Afghanistan. This is in stark contrast to 1988, when the wild poliovirus was endemic in more than 125 countries on five continents, paralyzing more than one thousand children every day.

During my term as president of Edina Rotary Club, India became polio-free in 2012, which made us extremely proud of all the efforts made by Rotarians around the world to eradicate this terrible disease.

Rotary International has been one of the most reliable partners of GPEI. Since 1988, more than two billion children around the world have been immunized against polio, thanks to the unprecedented cooperation of more than two hundred countries and twenty million volunteers. This project was also backed by an international investment of more than five billion dollars. More than a million Rotarians around the world have participated in this project.

According to Rotary International's website, in January 2009, Rotary International and the Bill & Melinda Gates Foundation announced a further joint financing commitment of several hundred million dollars toward the effort to eradicate polio. In the middle of a global financial crisis, additional significant funding was also announced by the governments of Germany and the United Kingdom.

Bill Gates once said, "Rotarians, government leaders, and health professionals have made a phenomenal commitment so polio afflicts only a small number of the world's children. Rotary in particular has inspired my own personal commitment to get deeply involved in achieving polio eradication." Apparently, Mr. Gates has been heavily influenced by his father, who has been a Rotarian for all his life.

I will never forget the following experience at one of our regular Rotary meetings in 1998. That year, Rotary International beefed up its efforts to eradicate polio and reduce the number of the afflicted, particularly in Africa. For this project, our president, Tom McNellis, thought of many different ways to raise funds among members. He came to the conclusion it would be best to invite a polio victim as a speaker.

The week before this scheduled speech, our second daughter, Maria, was born, so the meeting and its circumstances are still quite vivid in my memory. President Tom asked me to announce our daughter's birth at the beginning of the meeting. Then, as soon as various other announcements and lunch were over, he introduced our guest speaker. Tom said, "Today's speaker is Jerry." Then there was a long pause. The room all of a sudden became quiet. Tom choked up, unable to speak. He made all of us wonder why. After overcoming his emotions, he continued.

"As you all know, today's theme is polio eradication. Lately, the United Nations and Rotary International have been working together to eradicate polio around the world, and admittedly, they have made a lot of progress. However, polio still occurs in certain African and East Asian countries. So I thought we should invite a speaker who experienced polio and can tell us the importance of its prevention and eradication. Today's speaker is Jerry McNellis. He and I . . ." There was another pause. Tom choked up again, and we became more serious than before.

"Jerry and I grew up together. He is my brother. I remember how sick Jerry became after contracting polio. We were both elementary school kids. After he became sick, I didn't see him for a while. The doctor ordered him to be separated from the rest of us, so we wouldn't get the poliovirus from him. I missed playing with him, but there was nothing much I could do to change his situation. When we were reunited, Jerry's leg was not the same. He could not run as he did before, and we could not play with each other as we did before. Over the past forty years, I have asked God why he chose Jerry instead of me. Why did God choose Jerry instead of someone else?" Tom was overwhelmed by his own emotions again.

He continued, "A few weeks ago, I asked Jerry to come and speak for us at our club meeting. I was wondering whether he would consider accepting my invitation, but, to my surprise, he gladly accepted. I apologize for choking up today, despite my last night's resolution not to—I simply cannot help it when I introduce my brother. I asked him to come early, so no one in the audience could recognize his legs or his condition before his speech. So, ladies and gentlemen, here is today's speaker and my brother, Jerry."

To this date, I don't recall a more somber moment in my life than that day. We didn't know exactly why, but something in all of us told us we should give Jerry a big hand. As we began to clap our hands, Tom said, "Jerry, to maximize the effect of your condition, why don't you limp as you come to the podium?"

At this joke, the audience laughed, some with tears in their eyes. Jerry, who was sitting quietly at the rear end of the room, stood up, but he didn't move for a while. He said, "Tom, I agree with you. I should limp. But which leg do you want me to limp on?" We all laughed again, while applauding. Our applause continued until Jerry reached the podium.

Jerry shared his experience of growing up with polio, and we all agreed afterward that this was one of the best speeches we heard that year. As a result of Jerry's speech, we donated a lot of money to the Polio Eradication Project, to the excitement of our president, Tom. I don't remember every detail of his speech, but I remember his sense of humor and his remarkable ability to see the bright side of life, even in the face of seemingly insurmountable misfortune, which could have ruined his life. I also remember the big hug Tom and Jerry gave each other at the end of Jerry's speech. I knew that Tom hugged Jerry on behalf of all our club's members and guests in the audience.

Around Christmastime a few years ago, Tom called me out of the blue. He said to me that Jerry wrote a book based on his experience of growing up with polio. And before I knew it, Tom arranged to have an author-signed copy of the book sent to my office. The book was written by Jerry and his mother, and they were both candid about every aspect of Jerry's life. I was deeply touched by the fact that the family did its best to help Jerry pick himself up and never give up on him.

If we Rotarians succeed in eradicating polio in the last four remaining countries (now three, after India is officially removed from this list), then the word "polio" will disappear from all the dictionaries around the world. This project started more than twenty years ago, and 99 percent of the work is done, but the remaining 1 percent still remains a daunting task. It could be 2018, or even later, but we Rotarians know the end of polio is coming for sure. Sometimes I imagine a day when I will babysit my future grandchildren. I would like to tell them: "There once was a disease called polio. You may not even see it in the dictionary today. It used to kill or cripple one thousand kids daily around the world. Do you know how it disappeared? A few good people, called Rotarians, worked together to help eradicate it. You know what? I was one of them."

Proud members of Edina Rotary Club, who achieved 100 percent attendance during 2011–2012 Rotary year.

A Rotarian Taught Me
How to Pray

Kindness is a language which the deaf can hear and the blind can see.

—Mark Twain

When I feel down, I sing or hum Beatles' songs. Then, miraculously, I feel better. I like their lyrics because they comfort me.

"When I find myself in times of trouble, Mother Mary comes to me / Speaking words of wisdom, let it be / And in my hour of darkness, she is standing right in front of me / Speaking words of wisdom, let it be."

This is part of The Beatles' famous song titled "Let it Be." Do you have Mother Mary, or someone like her, who comes to visit you and show you the way out of trouble? I do. I have quite a few, as a matter of fact.

Since 2003, my life has been going very well. I haven't become sick for several years. Since 2003, I have had the most peaceful of relationships with my friends and relatives. Since 2003, I haven't received any speeding or parking tickets. Many good things happened in my life since 2003. For example, it was 2003 that I began to save money and started our two daughters' college funds.

Things have been going just great, and I began to feel proud of myself. But I hadn't realized until much later how much I owed my recent streak of happiness, luck, and success to the prayers of Bob Solheim, one of my fellow Rotarians. I had a strong realization recently that it is Bob who taught me how to appreciate life again. He taught me the meaning of the following prayer I glued to the corner of my desk:

> *The greatest joy in life is Giving.*
> *The most satisfying work is Helping Others.*
> *The most effective sleeping pill is Peace of mind.*
> *The most powerful force in life is Love.*
> *The greatest asset is Faith.*
> *The most beautiful attire is a Smile.*
> *The most contagious spirit is Enthusiasm.*
> *The post powerful channel of communication is Prayer.*

One morning in 2002, I could not wake up, or to be more precise, I didn't want to move at all. I didn't have the energy to speak, eat, or drink, either. My wife, Jennifer, had left for work already, and the kids were gone to school. I closed my eyes and fell asleep again. When I opened my eyes, it was ten o'clock in the morning. I skipped breakfast, but I didn't feel hungry at all.

The phone rang.

With a weak voice, I answered the phone. "Hello." It was Jennifer. She called me because she was worried about me.

"Wooj. Thank God. What are you doing home at this hour? I called your office, and there was no answer. Are you okay?"

" . . ."

"Wooj. Say something. Lately you don't seem to be yourself. Did you have some food? Why don't you go to see a doctor? Wooj, say something." Jennifer was genuinely worried.

In an attempt to assure her that I was okay, I faked a normal voice. "Jennifer, I am all right. I think I have a cold. I will go to see a doctor this afternoon."

We hung up the phone. As much as I wanted to have a comforting conversation with Jennifer, somehow I didn't want to reveal my most vulnerable moment to her.

I could not find the cause of the problem, although I knew there were a few things that bothered me a great deal. First of all, I had too many cases in my office. I had clients who demanded too much from me. I also lost a lot of money in the stock market, which made me feel ashamed and sorry toward my family. I had personally invested in two companies where the partners were close friends of mine, but the investments didn't go as well as I expected, adding more stress and misery to my already complicated life.

It was depression that made me weak. I didn't realize that all the minor fluctuations around me were leading to this condition. Soon I began to spend nights without any sleep at all, and there were many days when I slept in and didn't feel like getting up or going to work. I admit I took sleeping pills sometimes, but they didn't help me much. I had some physical ailments too. After spending several weeks like this, I realized I had lost about twenty pounds.

Deep down, I felt genuinely sad and miserable. When I didn't feel like going to work, I called my secretary and said I had a cold. I told her to take messages if there were any from those "difficult" clients. I just didn't want to meet anyone.

Occasionally I went to my office to work, but after responding to a few phone calls, I would decide to leave early. I drove aimlessly. I drove along the Mississippi River. I crossed the same bridge three times, back and forth. I went to a department store and walked for hours without buying anything. I went to a lake and sat on a bench to look at the people, who all seemed to be happy and enjoying life. Then I drove through the most expensive neighborhood, where "happy" people were living in "happy" houses. I thought how lucky these folks must be, living in such fortresses.

Then one morning I could not bear it any longer, so I began to call every friend I knew in town, including a few Rotarians, in random order. Some of them were too busy or not interested in what I had to say. After all, we didn't become brothers and sisters by joining Rotary. Then Bob Solheim answered the phone. He somehow sensed the serious nature of my call immediately. He offered to have breakfast with me the next morning.

As soon as he saw me, Bob held my hand and told me that he decided to see me because I reminded him of his predicament thirty years ago. Contrary to what I thought of him, he also had his share of difficult moments, as well, when he was younger. He told me I should not take life too seriously under any circumstance. He said, "Wooj, call me at any time. I will sit with you again and again. We are both Rotarians, and it means we should help each other if there is any such need." As we said goodbye, he said he would pray for me. I thanked him. The fact that every man—regardless of his race, nationality, origin, religion, or education—at one point or another will go through difficult times in his life provided me with a great sense of relief and comfort. Bob's message that I was not alone in something like this comforted me greatly.

When I could not bear this depression any longer, I finally decided to go to see a doctor. I met Dr. Smith. He said I needed to do him a favor by following his instructions, which were something like the following:

1. Go home. 2. Get a piece of paper and pencil. 3. Draw a vertical line on the paper. 4. In the left column, write what I must do to live my life. 5. In the right column, write what I don't have to do. 6. Try to focus on what I must do (left column), and say NO to what I don't have to do (right column).

At the beginning, I thought he was a quack, and I didn't feel like following his Life 101-type of advice. However, since I didn't know of any other immediate way to improve my life, I gradually began to follow his advice. When I did everything he told me to do, slowly but miraculously, my life began to regain some order. Convinced that his advice was good, I decided to quit my membership with all social organizations but Rotary Club, which was too near and dear to my heart.

With the free time I gained by quitting my membership with all of the organizations, I began to read Viktor Frankl's book, *Man's Search for Meaning*, and ended up reading it five times in a row. After feeling the extraordinary impact the book had on me, I began to recommend this book to people around me, including one inmate in Sherburne County jail, and another client who faced extreme financial difficulties. They all told me the book was very helpful in coping with the down side of their lives.

Viktor Frankl claimed that man should find meaning in his life in the face of the most insurmountable obstacles, such as guilt, pain, or death. The fact that he survived a Nazi concentration camp with a strong will and reason to live—he could not die without seeing his immediate family members, who were in another concentration camp—made me realize that all my troubles were so trivial compared to his, and I had every reason to overcome my troubles and move on with my life.

Frankl also argued that we human beings could derive meaning of life from various sources, such as love, work, and suffering. I could understand love and work, but I didn't understand why he would list "suffering" as a source of meaning in life. According to Frankl, there are two reasons why suffering can be a source of meaning. Firstly, because of our "spiritual freedom" to choose the *attitude* we have toward things around us, we can choose which attitude to take to our suffering, as well. Secondly, we can choose to see suffering as our "task" and transform it into victory. Frankl quotes Fyodor Dostoyevsky, who once said, "There is only one thing that I dread: not to be worthy of my sufferings." Essentially, suffering enables us to turn it into "an achievement"—which transforms a personal tragedy into a triumph.

Whenever I recommended this book, virtually everyone was moved by it. Many of my friends told me that they were all awed by the author's keen insight into the meaning of suffering in our lives.

About six years passed since I met and overcame the big crisis in my life, and I happened to sit next to Bob Solheim at one of our weekly Rotary Club meetings. After exchanging routine pleasantries, Bob said, "Wooj, did you know that I have been praying for you every day for the past six years?" My jaw dropped and I looked into his eyes. All of a sudden, I realized that Bob was my "Mother Mary" who showed me the way out of trouble and in the right direction. I realized that he was the wind beneath my wings, and he was the one who supported me every time I needed the power to face life's bumps over the past six years.

After realizing and witnessing the power of prayer Bob gave me, these days I try to remember at least one person I meet during the day and include him or her in my prayer before I go to bed. I am not sure whether I am as patient as Bob, who prayed on my behalf for the past six years, but I think it is my duty to return the power of prayer back to someone who may need it urgently.

Years ago, a friend of mine sent the following prayer to me. I try to recite it before I go to bed, thinking of a person who may need it:

Dear Lord,
Here is my brain—think with it.
Here is my face—smile through it.
Here is my tongue—speak to people with it.
Here is my ear—listen to people with it.
Here is my hand—touch someone with it.
Here are my arms—lift and hug someone with them.
Here are my feet—walk with them where you want to go today.
Please help me become a serving person.

Moses Miracle

> In life, what truly matters is not what we bought, but what we built; not what we received, but what we shared; not our competence, but our character; and not our success, but our significance. Live a life that matters. Live a life of love.
>
> —Anonymous

I believe it was sometime in March 2010 when Edina Rotarian Sandy Schley called me and suggested that our two daughters come to her house to play violin for a boy, named Moses Mwaura, who would receive a life-changing surgery the next day. She said she decided to throw a party for this boy, who came all the way from a slum in Kenya to Minnesota to correct his crossed eyes and straighten his crooked teeth. When we arrived at Sandy's house, there were about fifty people there, including Rotarian Jim Hovland, the mayor of Edina. Nina and Maria played violin for almost two hours and played with this six-year-old boy from Africa.

I have known Sandy for a long time as one of my trusted Rotary mentors. While serving as the governor of Rotary International District 5950, which covers a large part of Minnesota, she went to

Africa a few times, mainly to work on a project whose purpose was to bring clean water to needy people in East Africa. When she was touring a small town, called the Mathare Valley, she ran into Moses, the youngest of four children of a single mother in a slum.

When Sandy bumped into this boy, all of a sudden, she felt a strong surge of pain. His face was covered by flies, and his eyes were terribly crossed, which made it difficult for him to see anything straight. When she came back to Minnesota, even though it looked like an almost impossible mission, Sandy began to discuss the possibility of fixing this African boy's crossed eyes. When Dr. Chuck Barer, who is also a Rotarian, heard this discussion, he suggested that his associate, Dr. Jafar Hasan, could perform the surgery on the boy, if and only if the boy could come to Minnesota.

Sandy began to worry about the next question: Who will bring the boy from Africa to Minnesota? Thankfully, another Rotarian, Tim Murphy, who usually raises his hand when there is no volunteer in the room, volunteered to do this job. The next question was: Who will pay for his trip? Rotarian Tom Bach mobilized his employer, Delta Airlines, to donate tickets for the boy. Eden Prairie Rotarian Dr. Angela Waganda offered to straighten the boy's crooked teeth.

Soon, this chain of reaction and instantaneous collaboration by and among the Rotarians became known as "the Miracle of Moses," which touched the hearts of people not only in Minnesota but also people in Kenya, as well.

Dr. Hasan operated on Moses's badly crossed eyes, a condition he probably was born with. Dr. Hasan cut and reattached the inside muscles of both eyes to straighten them. The surgery went very well. Dr. Waganda fixed Moses's crooked teeth while he was still under anesthesia.

Three days after the surgery, Moses, still recovering, came to our weekly club meeting. Our club members finally saw the small boy who was the subject of big miracle in this small town. Toward the end of the year, our club's board decided to raise money for Moses's education in Kenya. Basically, Edina Rotarians decided to fully stand behind this miracle started by Sandy Schley. Toward the end of 2010, Edina Rotary raised more than $29,000, which was a sufficient amount for Moses Mwaura's education from kindergarten to college in Kenya.

When Mother Teresa was invited to the International Rotary Convention in 1981, in São Paulo, Brazil, she said to the Rotary audience: "If we really want to love, if we really want to live, then we must love until it hurts. No Rotarian whose motto is 'service above self' should call himself a Rotarian if he does not make time to serve."

The Moses Miracle created by Rotarians, including Sandy Schley, is a good example of what Mother Teresa meant by "service above self." The Moses Miracle happened because, in my opinion, Rotarian Sandy Schley felt the pain of the boy in her heart, and she turned that pain into love, which then triggered service above self in many Rotarians.

Moses was taken care of by Sandy Schley and Cindy Murphy (with glasses) while he received surgeries in Minnesota. I believe the Moses Miracle was born because Sandy Schley felt pain and love for this boy, which is comparable to an oyster painfully growing pearl in its soft flesh. (Photo Credit: MN Dental Association)

Chinese President's Iowa Rotary Visit

The road to a friend's house is never too far.
—Norwegian Proverb

Recently, the president-elect of Edina Rotary Club, Jeff Ohe, invited the University of Minnesota president, Eric Kaler, to our club. President Kaler delivered a state-of-the-art speech about the university, which produces fine graduates and sends them to work all over the world. According to him, China's minister of agriculture is a graduate of the University of Minnesota.

Mr. Kaler's story reminded me of an article I happened to read in *The Wall Street Journal*. According to the newspaper (January 31, 2012), a small Iowan city, called Muscatine, was to host Xi Jinping, China's then president-elect. This was Mr. Xi's second visit to the town since 1985. For his first visit, Mr. Xi, then a low-ranking official in a rural region in China, led an animal-feed delegation to Iowa. He toured farms, visited a Rotary Club, and watched a baseball game. He also spent two nights in the split-level home of a Muscatine couple, sleeping with the Star Trek toys on display in their children's bedroom. Apparently it was Mr. Xi's first trip outside China, and needless to say, he was quite impressed by this small city's hospitality.

On February 15, 2012, one day after he visited the White House for the first time to meet with President Obama, Mr. Xi flew to Muscatine, Iowa, and shared tea with the people he met in 1985, who included Rotarians. In fact, the Rotarians of Muscatine greeted him in exactly the same way as they greeted him three decades ago.

I often share this kind of story with my fellow Rotary Club members. I tell them to be nice to whoever sits next to them! He/she may become the next president of a country or company, which may turn the world around. Apparently, largely due to efforts made by those farmers and Rotarians who treated Mr. Xi with exceptional hospitality during his first visit, Iowan farmers today export their products to China in excess of six hundred million dollars annually. We can safely assume that the number will continue to increase since Mr. Xi became the president of China in 2013. The Rotarians in Iowa, who believed in world peace and goodwill, and showed Iowa-style hospitality to this humble young Chinese bureaucrat, were very wise people. The seeds they planted in the form of kindness and hospitality are paying off today.

Over the past two decades, I had the honor of sitting next to many guests from all over the world who visited our club. They came from Finland, Japan, Germany, Sweden, England, France, Nigeria, Korea, and across the United States, just to name a few. I hope we sent them off with good hospitality and friendship. I believe we Rotarians are in the business of helping the world become a better place because we welcome visitors from other parts of the world and speak about service above self, like the Rotarians in Iowa did three decades ago when Mr. Xi Jinping visited them.

These two ambassadorial scholars came to visit us on my first day as president of Edina Rotary Club in July 2011. They are Anna Ueda from Osaka, Japan, and Ann Heinzerling, who is from Minnesota and went to London, England, to study with a Rotary Ambassadorial Scholarship from our district. I always met these ambassadorial scholars with a great sense of honor and pleasure.

Who knows—they may become a great leader in the future.

We Shall Meet Again

Do not follow where the path may lead you. Go instead
where there is no path, and leave a trail.

—Anonymous

It has been our club's tradition to send our incoming president to
attend the Rotary International Convention before the new Rotary
year starts in July. So, in May 2011, the Rotary Club of Edina sent
me to New Orleans, where the Rotary International Convention
took place.

As soon as I boarded the plane in the Minneapolis/Saint
Paul Airport, which was Delta Air Line's major hub, I began to
see people from Hong Kong, Japan, Kenya, France, California,
Wisconsin, and Iowa, as well as Minnesota. I could tell that the
plane was exuberant with the Rotarians' happy spirits. They all
greeted each other, totally transcending their individual differences
and as if they had been friends for a long time. The gentleman
sitting next to me flew from Japan. He said he was coming from
Miyagi Prefecture, which was hit hard by the 2011 tsunami. He said
he almost gave up the trip, but he changed his mind as his club's
members told him that he should go to the international convention

and convey the message to all the Rotarians around the world that his club, his city, and his country will overcome the disaster. I was deeply touched by his humbleness, resolve, and courage.

I told him that I was reading Mother Teresa's biography, and I showed him the page where there was a prayer by her:

> Lord, make a channel of Thy peace that, where there is hatred, I may bring love; that, where there is wrong, I may bring the spirit of forgiveness; that, where there is discord, I may bring harmony; that, where there is error, I may bring truth; that, where there is doubt, I may bring faith; that, where there is despair, I may bring hope; that, where there are shadows, I may bring light; that, where there is sadness, I may bring joy.

I told him that I was sorry about the disaster in his country and that our club will find a way to help his club in Japan, for which he thanked me profusely.

During the convention, I had a chance to meet and associate with more than twenty thousand Rotarians and their family members from all over the world. I was glad to discover that the conference took place in New Orleans. It was supposed to be the host city for Rotary International's convention a few years back. But because of Hurricane Katrina, Rotary International had to cancel the convention. About five years later, Rotarians decided to keep their promise to convene again in this city of jazz.

According to Rotary International's estimate, in just four days, we Rotarians spent in New Orleans more than $200 million, which the city's weakened economy desperately needed in the aftermath of Hurricane Katrina. Many interesting Rotarians from different parts of the world all showed a genuine willingness to discuss ways to change the world into a better place. Our main plenary session's keynote speaker was Bill Gates, who committed more than five hundred million dollars to Rotary's Polio Plus project. He honored us by saying that he could not think of any better partner than Rotary International in fighting diseases and poverty in underdeveloped countries and that he gladly chose Rotary's polio eradication project as the beneficiary of his matching fund. He also said that he was deeply touched by the fact that we Rotarians already collected more than two billion dollars to eradicate polio in the past twenty years. After his speech, we gave him a standing ovation for a few minutes. I thought his speech truly declared and sealed the union of the most generous two organizations in the world: Rotary International and Bill & Melinda Gates Foundation.

As I was leaving the auditorium after Bill Gates's speech, I heard a group of people speaking in the dialect of Busan, my hometown in Korea. The room was still dark and I could not see them clearly, but I was drawn to them. When the room was lit again, I could see their faces. They were forty Rotarians from Busan. When I introduced myself to them, one of them seemed to recognize me. "Are you the young student we gave the scholarship to twenty years ago?" When I said yes, they all cheered and we gave each other a big hug. Without a moment's hesitation, we decided to continue our conversation at dinner.

During dinner, these Korean Rotarians were very curious about my life in the United States.

"Is Minnesota a good place?"

"Do people treat you well?"

"Is it good to become president of the second largest club in District 5950?"

"Are Scandinavians nice people?"

To all these questions, I gave only one simple answer: "You betcha!"

I thanked the Rotarians again for investing $23,800 in me twenty years ago. I said, "We all met Bill Gates earlier today. Instead of giving me a scholarship, you could have invested the same amount of money in Microsoft, in which case, you would be sitting on a two million-dollar return today. I always wanted to pay back Rotary, and the Rotarians in Edina thought that I should become a Rotarian instead of paying back the money. I still ask myself the question: Which one should I pay back to Rotary International—the original $23,800 or $2 million, which is the original investment's return today?"

Then, one Rotarian from Busan said, "The scholarship was a gift from us to you. We never expected you to pay back. In addition, you already achieved more than a two million-dollar return for us anyway by becoming a Rotarian. Look at yourself. Not only becoming a Rotarian, you became a multiple Paul Harris Fellow. Now you are becoming the president of one of the most prestigious Rotary Clubs in the United States. How much more can we expect from a scholarship recipient? We are just glad to see you here."

Over dinner, I choked up several times, marveling at the circle becoming full in my humble world. The forty Rotarians from Busan kept giving me words of encouragement and wisdom, knowing that I would become the president of the best Rotary Club in the United States in just one month!

During the remaining three days of the convention, we met several times, and on the last day, we went on a river cruise tour together, as well. I told the Rotarians from Busan that I met many Korean War veterans and Korean adoptees in Minnesota. One Rotarian said that there must be some connection between the Mississippi River in Minnesota and the Nakdong River in Busan. Speaking of Nakdong, this river was the last defense line for tens of thousands of US soldiers—soldiers such as Bill Clynes, Milt Adams, Harold Harris, Ron Erhardt, and Paul Zerby, whom I meet regularly in Minnesota—who served in the US military before and during the Korean War to defend South Korea from the invading communist soldiers of North Korea in early 1950s. The Korean Rotarians and I spoke about the interesting connection between Minnesota and Korea.

On my way back to Minnesota, I thought to myself that this circle becoming full in my humble life all started with Rotary. After all, were it not for the scholarship, I don't think I would have had the opportunity to broaden my horizons. Were it not for the Rotary Club of Edina, who funded my trip to New Orleans, I would not have had the opportunity to attend the convention and meet with the Korean Rotarians who gave me the scholarship more than twenty years ago.

The trip to New Orleans definitely contributed to my resolution to become one of the best presidents the Edina Rotary Club has ever seen. This trip also made me realize that we live in a small world, known as one global Rotary community.

I attended the Rotary International Convention in New Orleans in May of 2011, where I met Rotarians from Korea who gave me a scholarship in 1990.

Lessons I Learned
from Rotarians

You are not here merely to make a living. You are here to enable the world to live more amply, with greater vision, with a finer spirit of hope and achievement. You are here to enrich the world and you impoverish yourself if you forget the errand.

—Woodrow Wilson

A few years ago, a check was delivered to our house. The amount was roughly four hundred dollars, and it came from our two daughters' school district. Initially, I was quite puzzled as to why the school would send us any money, but it didn't take much time for me to discover the reason. After transferring our daughters from the Saint Paul public school district to the Edina school district on an open enrollment basis (which allows children living out of the school district to attend the school within the district), we were still living out of the district for one year before we moved to Edina. The honorable school district of Edina, knowing that we were burning extra gas to bring our kids to its district, decided to reimburse us for the extra cost of gas. This was when gas was above three dollars per gallon, and the total came to something like four hundred dollars in one year. I was impressed by the generous efforts the school district made to encourage and embrace children from outside their district to add more diversity to its student body. Since then, we moved to Edina, so this was the only year we received such a check from the school district.

Now I began to have many happy thoughts about what I could possibly purchase with this windfall money. A new thirty-two-inch flat-panel TV looked very attractive. My wife thought of some furniture for the house. Our two kids wanted iPods. Then I found a good place to put this money. Two Rotarians showed me the way.

Dr. Bob Margolis is a professor at the University of Minnesota Medical School. He is a member of the University of Minnesota Rotary Club, where everyone seems to be a scholar. This club boasts of 100 percent Paul Harris Fellowships. The club's meetings always start with a feature called "Brag for a Buck" which means that a member (or a guest) can brag about a special event during the week, after paying a dollar to the club. For a relatively small Rotary Club, I think this is a fantastic way of fundraising while promoting friendship among members.

I believe it was in either July or August 2008 when I attended a meeting at this club. Many people, including myself, bragged about our life's happy moments for that particular week. I put a dollar bill in the basket and said that I was happy about the windfall of four hundred dollars from our children's school district. When Dr. Margolis stood up, instead of putting a dollar in the basket, which usually is the case with other members, he turned in a white envelope, which made us all curious. He then provided an explanation. Apparently, he received a refund check from the IRS, which came to all American families in 2008, as a result of President Bush's economic stimulus package.

He said, "My wife and I don't need this money. There are many people who will benefit from this, so we decided to donate it to Rotary."

When I saw what Dr. Margolis did, I was deeply moved and ashamed at the same time. I decided to ask him a question after the meeting was over. I said, "Bob, I was impressed by what you said today. I have a question for you, though: Why didn't you cash the check and donate a smaller amount?"

Dr. Margolis said, "I am only human. If I had cashed it, then I might have changed my mind in the meantime, and my donating spirit might have diminished or disappeared entirely. I didn't want that to happen." Once again, he moved me.

At this point, I need to add a little note on Dr. Margolis. He is one of the founding members of International Hearing Foundation (IHF), which was instrumental in launching a special school in Santiago, Chile, for hearing-impaired children.

According to its website, IHF was founded in 1984 to support hearing-related services, education, and research around the world. It has sponsored teams of doctors that have traveled to Senegal, Peru, Brazil, Chile, and Cuba. These teams have volunteered their time and services doing operations, treating patients in clinics, and teaching local doctors about modern day treatments for ear conditions. In each of these trips, IHF has donated much needed medical supplies. Since IHF helped to create a deaf school in Chile, Rotary became a close partner.

At Dr. Margolis's recommendation, I have been donating money to this organization, and at my recommendation, Edina Rotary Club also became a partner of this project. As I recall, Dr. Margolis and his colleagues invited several medical staff members from Santiago, Chile, to Minneapolis and held conferences on deafness. I remember how deeply touched I was when I was invited to one such conference a few years ago.

Ever since I first met Dr. Margolis, I have been watching him very closely, and I have come to a conclusion that those who are generous with their time and money are living a life of abundance. In other words, people like him carry a well of generosity in their hearts, which never runs dry.

Here is another Rotarian who taught me where to donate the windfall money by deeply moving me about the same time. Joel Jennings, a member of Edina Rotary Club, became level two major donor by giving a $25,000 donation to the Rotary Foundation. He said, "My donation comes from abundance, and abundance is a matter of choice. Since I chose to live a life of abundance, I am HAPPY both before and after this donation. In fact, both abundance and happiness are a matter of choice for me."

I shared these two Rotarians' anecdotes with my family members, and we all agreed that we should give our four hundred dollar check from the school district to the Rotary Foundation.

I received the "Service above Self" award from Rotary District 5950 in 2008. The person giving me the award is Edina Rotary President Paul Mooty. (Photo Credit: Jennifer Bennerotte.)

Who Needs a Speaker?

> The other day I dreamed that I was at the gates of heaven.
> ... And Saint Peter said, "Go back to Earth. There are no
> slums up here."
>
> —Mother Teresa

The worst nightmare of a Rotary Club president is the scheduled
speaker not showing up at the weekly meeting. I am glad it didn't
happen to our club during my term as president; however, I heard
it happens at many other clubs for a variety of reasons. It could
be due to a bad weather or a flat tire or a family emergency on
the speaker's part. If the speaker's disgruntled wife decides to put
a small amount of poison in the speaker's breakfast or coffee, the
speaker may have to cancel his Rotary speech in the afternoon.
If he starts his day from the wrong side of the bed and slips and
breaks his hipbone, he may have to cancel the scheduled speech,
too. Emergencies do happen. Knowing this very well during my
term, on every Thursday morning, as soon as I woke up, I prayed
that our scheduled speaker didn't have an accident throughout the
entire day. Sometimes I wondered if I should discuss a plan B with
our board members to better prepare for this kind of disaster. But,

I didn't have such an opportunity to do so until I finished my term with luck on my side.

I attended a Rotary Club meeting once where the speaker didn't show up. And here is my memory of what happened.

Richfield is a neighboring city to Edina. I live less than a mile away from this city, but I never had a chance to attend a Rotary Club meeting there until after I became the president of our club. Richfield is a relatively small city, and the Rotary Club is also small, compared to the clubs in other neighboring cities.

The meeting at Champps restaurant started very casually. The restaurant was not yet open, but a few waitresses showed up to set up the tables and serve breakfast for the Richfield Rotarians. The president (a financial planner named Steve Larson) introduced two visiting Rotarians, including me, and made an apologetic announcement that the scheduled speaker didn't show up. Since I became president of our club, I just panicked at this news, even though it was not our club, nor was the meeting my responsibility. I felt a strong surge of sympathy for Steve. However, to my surprise, Steve was much calmer than I was. A couple of members (all very calm, too) went to whisper some ideas into Steve's ears. After a few minutes, Steve said, "Well, Rotarians, as we know it very well from our own lives, emergencies do happen. Since we don't have a speaker this morning, why don't we take time for our Happy Bucks?"

With this announcement, members began to talk about their happy moments. Each member contributed one dollar per happy occasion that he/she shared with other club members. One member spoke about recently becoming a grandmother. Another spoke about a promotion in his job. Another stood up and said he was just "happy" for no tangible reason. One member said he was happy because he was still healthy enough to walk to the Rotary Club meetings. To everybody's surprise, the club collected as much as forty dollars from the members in the name of "Happy Bucks." Steve later told me that, this way, the club ends up collecting as much as two to three thousand dollars during the year, and that most of the money goes to fund scholarships for needy children in the area. What a great idea!

As far as I recall, in our own club, a speaker not showing up happened only once in my eighteen-year membership history. On that day, we finished lunch and patiently waited for the speaker. When it became obvious that he would not show up, the president had to declare that the meeting was over. So we said goodbye to each other and hoped that it would never happen again. Indeed, it has never happened again.

Perhaps it helps to be small. Since Richfield Rotary Club is a small enough club, it is flexible enough to quickly change the meeting's format to an emergency mode. At Steve's suggestion, the members took turns talking about their happy moments and taught me that there were twenty different reasons to wake up on every Thursday morning in the city of Richfield. Steve also gave me a chance to talk about our club's upcoming fundraising events. Since he told me we had plenty of time, I made a long announcement.

I noticed that many Richfield Rotary members were curious about my background. I am sure they have seen plenty of members from our club, who all had a Scandinavian or European background. I explained my background, why I came to visit them, and why I wanted them to purchase the raffle tickets to help our annual fundraising. To my surprise, every member purchased the raffle tickets I presented to them, and I thanked them profusely. They filled not only their Happy Bucks basket, but also my envelope, as well. I still vividly remember how happy I was to meet the members of this small Rotary Club.

I strongly believe that Rotarians share certain DNA (I call this "service above self DNA"), regardless of the location or size of the club or the format of their meeting. I clearly saw this service DNA in the morning of September 22, 2011, when I visited Richfield Rotary Club. I didn't have a chance to listen to the planned speaker; however, twenty Rotarians shared their own "happiness" stories with me and made me happy. They had the wisdom to turn the emergency into such a positive occasion so that, toward the end of the meeting, we all completely forgot about the scheduled speaker. Maybe the speaker, who overslept that morning or was poisoned by his wife, blessed this club by not showing up that morning. I had a simple goal when I set out to visit Richfield Rotary Club on that morning: selling raffle tickets for our club's fundraising. But I came back with a bag of happiness that lasted for several months. Long live Richfield Rotary! Long live Happy Bucks! Long live the speaker who didn't show up!

Former Minnesota Governor Arne Carlson came to speak at our club in 2012. Next to him is Charlie Weigel, president of Edina Morningside Rotary Club.

Feed My Starving Children

Too often we underestimate the power of a touch, a smile,
a kind word, a listening ear, an honest compliment, or the
smallest act of caring, all of which have the potential to
turn a life around.

—Leo Buscaglia

Takashi Yanase (1919–2013), creator of one of Japan's most be-
loved cartoon characters, called Anpanman, has died of heart fail-
ure at the age of ninety-four. Anpanman is a superhero with a head
made of "anpan," which is bread filled with red bean paste, a very
typical and delicious snack in Asia. The round-faced, smiley hero,
clad in a red suit and long cape (just like Superman in America),
became hugely popular in a picture book series that started in 1969.
The Anpanman television cartoon series started in 1988 and has
spread to the rest of Asia. It is still featured on Japan's national TV,
and I have been enjoying this cartoon greatly.

When he was in his early twenties, Yanase participated in the
China-Japan War as a soldier, and he saw famine's garish face.
Both soldiers and civilians starved to death. When he saw inno-
cent children dying of hunger, he came to a conclusion that bread

for an individual human being, regardless of the individual's background, was more important than justice for a society or victory for a country. Based on his first-hand experience of hunger, he created Anpanman, who basically flies to wherever people need bread. His message was well received by people all over the world. Apparently, his books sold more than sixty million copies.

When Brad Beard decided to join Edina Rotary Club, our club's board members were extremely happy. He was president of Fairview Southdale Hospital, the biggest hospital in our city. Our club's board members were increasingly tired of too many membership applications submitted by people in one profession—financial planners—when there seemed no money left to be planned about anyway, due to a terrible global economic recession of 2008. Rotary International has been encouraging club leaders to diversify the club's membership, and, needless to say, Brad's job classification was a good one for our club. When I heard that he was interested in fighting hunger by joining Rotary, I somehow knew that we recruited a good man.

Paul Mooty, one of my Rotary mentors, lost his father. At the funeral service, I happened to sit next to Brad Beard. When Brad asked me how I was doing, I told him Maria, our second daughter, just broke her leg and that we needed to get a pair of crutches during her recovery. The funeral service started soon after, and we could not talk any more. Brad took a piece of paper out of his pocket and wrote his home address on it. Then he whispered, "Wooj, come pick up the crutches any time from this afternoon. I will leave them outside our front door." I whispered back to him, "Thank you."

Two years later, Maria, an avid dancer, broke her leg again, and we borrowed the crutches again from Brad. Each time, Brad was most caring and generous. (When Maria broke her leg the second time, we also borrowed a wheelchair from Rotarian Bob Solheim, too, without which Maria's recovery would have been more difficult.)

I discovered that, despite his busy schedule as the president of the biggest hospital in our city, Brad turned out to be one of the most dedicated Rotarians. About four years ago, our club's board discussed whether we could invite some doctors from area hospitals to our club, who could share their expertise with us on subjects including the heart, kidneys, and cancer. As I recall, Brad arranged at least ten doctors from his hospital to come to our club, who were all experts in their individual areas. After meeting with ten brilliant medical doctors, our club members definitely became more knowledgeable about how to live a healthy and fulfilling life. These top-notch doctors spent their professional hours just to share their expertise with Rotarians, and it was possible all because of Brad's connection and convincing skills.

When the board asked Brad whether he was interested in becoming the chair of a local project, known as Feed My Starving Children (FMSC), without a moment's hesitation, Brad took the job and began to regularly and diligently organize Edina Rotary members to go to FMSC's venue in Chanhassen, Minnesota, to package meals for starving children around the world.

When I asked my family members to volunteer for this project organized by Brad Beard, they all said YES. After being sufficiently impressed by Brad's efforts to help FMSC, I asked my secretary to join in this project, too, and she showed up with her daughter, who just entered kindergarten.

So what is Feed My Starving My Children anyway? According to its website, it was established in 1987 as a nonprofit organization for the purpose of eliminating starvation in children throughout the world by helping to instill compassion in people to hear and respond to the cries of those in need. Challenged by needs he had seen on missions in Honduras, in 1982 Minnesota businessman Richard Proudfit heard God say to him one day, "If you have seen my starving children, feed them." In early 1987, he incorporated Feed My Starving Children to develop an original meal formula. Then Cargill food scientist Dr. Richard Fulmer teamed up with a scientist at Pillsbury and General Mills, and together they came up with a rice formula called "MannaPack," which is a nutritious and fortified rice-soy combination casserole sufficient enough to satisfy a hungry child. The question of how the food should be packed was solved when Green Giant donated more than one million plastic bags from a discontinued product.

When all these logistical issues were taken care of, the

organization needed volunteers who could package the food, which would be delivered to hungry children all over the world.

During my most recent visit to FMSC, I discovered some interesting statistics:

- Of six hundred million meals shipped, 99.96 percent have reached the hungry children they were originally meant for.

- Meals cost only twenty-two cents each. Just eighty dollars feeds a child for a year!

- FMSC's three-meal formulas are packed with soy protein, dried vegetables, and twenty vitamins and minerals—everything needed for a malnourished child to recover.

With the advent of digital technology, we can locate any city around the world by just turning on a GPS. But no sophisticated machine can tell us who is starving in that city. And we know for sure that there are children starving virtually everywhere. That is why we need an organization like FMSC and that is why Rotarians volunteer to pack and send meals for starving children around the world.

The beneficiaries of these packaged meals live in many places, such as the deserts of Afghanistan, the trash heaps of Nicaragua, and the scrap huts of Haiti. I found the following story on FMSC's website, written by Mark Crea, its executive director:

> Pierre and his older brother were left in the care of their father, who could not feed the boys. Nearly one year old, Pierre was only twelve pounds and near death when he was rushed to a hospital for treatment for worms, scabies, and severe malnourishment. He was discharged to Mission Haiti Helping Kids (an orphanage) where he began to eat the packaged meals sent by Feed My Starving Children. The orphanage gets 3,240 meals every month to feed its thirty children, including Pierre!

Every month, Love A Child (LAC) receives six cargo containers from FMSC—1.6 million meals. After paying shipping costs, LAC gives nearly a half-million meals to forty smaller missions, including <u>Mission Haiti Helping Kids</u>. The food nourishes clinics, children's homes, schools, and street ministries all across the island of Haiti.

Edina Rotary Club has been a partner/sponsor of this project for the past few years. It became a family project for us twice a year. It is humble to know that we can feed starving children around the world with a meal which costs less than twenty-five cents.

Do Good Anyway

My grandfather once told me that there were two kinds
of people: those who do the work and those who take the
credit. He told me to try to be in the first group; there was
much less competition.

—Indira Gandhi

Did it ever occur to you that every time you want to watch TV,
you cannot find the remote control to turn it on? It happens to me
all the time. When I told him it happens to me frequently, Ben, a
former Rotarian friend of mine, shared the following joke, which
kind of consoled me. It is about our forgetfulness of important
things around us:

> With the miracle of fertility treatment, a woman was
> able to have a baby at the age of sixty-five.
> When she was discharged from hospital, her relatives
> came to visit.
> "Can we see the baby?" they asked.
> "Not yet," said the sixty-five-year-old mother.
> Twenty minutes later, they asked again, "Can we see the
> baby?"

"Not yet," said the mother.

Another twenty minutes later, they asked again, "Can we see the baby?"

"Not yet," said the mother.

Growing very impatient, they said, "Well, when can we see the baby then?"

"When it cries."

"Why do we have to wait until the baby cries?"

"Because I forgot where I put it."

During my term as president of Edina Rotary Club, I had the opportunity to discuss "service" with new Rotarians, and I shared this joke. We know for sure that there is a baby out there somewhere, but because the baby is not crying yet, we just don't see it, and we tend to forget that there is a baby. Likewise, we know for sure that there are people who need our service, but we just don't see them every day, and we tend to let that "service" slip to the bottom of our to-do list. There are millions of needy people around the world, but we are too busy to recognize their need. The need could be found in a remote village in another continent or in a family around the corner in our neighborhood. Those who join service organizations, such as Rotary, become aware of these needs, and they get ready to fill the gap in the forgotten or damaged chain of help pipeline, where the government or a big corporation alone cannot possibly meet all the needs of the people both in the local and global community.

"But why should I give my money to a remote village in Africa when I know that my own neighbors are suffering in this bad economy? Why should I roll up my sleeves in anticipation of all the disasters around the world, which may be too big for me to handle anyway?" I often hear this kind of comment from new members or those who procrastinate joining Rotary. I felt the same way for a while, to tell the truth, even after joining Rotary, until one day when I heard the invocation of Bill Carter, one of my fellow Rotarians and also one of the best plastic surgeons in town.

He went to South America to perform surgeries on cleft-lipped children on a pro bono basis. He shared the following invocation with us at the beginning of one of our regular meetings:

> *Anyway*
> *People are unreasonable, illogical, and self-centered.*
> *LOVE THEM ANYWAY.*
> *If you do good, people will accuse you of selfish, ulterior motive.*
> *DO GOOD ANYWAY.*
> *If you are successful, you win false friends and true enemies.*
> *SUCCEED ANYWAY.*
> *The good you do will be forgotten tomorrow.*
> *DO GOOD ANYWAY.*
> *Honesty and frankness make you vulnerable.*
> *BE HONEST AND FRANK ANYWAY.*
> *What you spent years building may be destroyed overnight.*
> *BUILD ANYWAY.*
> *People really need help but may attack you if you help them.*
> *HELP PEOPLE ANYWAY.*
> *Give the world the best you have and you will get kicked in the teeth.*
> *GIVE THE WORLD THE BEST YOU'VE GOT ANYWAY.*

I discovered later this is either a quotation from Mother Teresa or an anonymous scripture written somewhere in an orphanage in Calcutta, where Mother Teresa worked.

Before I joined Rotary (and for a while even after receiving the scholarship from Rotary, I admit), I always had the tendency to expect recognition every time I offered any service. Sometimes I was not sure whether it was such a good idea to raise money and send it to Africa when we had suffering neighbors in our own neighborhood. But now, I try to, and often actually, provide service above self ANYWAY, regardless of the beneficiary's location or background, if I am given an opportunity to do so, simply for the sake of giving. This is perhaps one of the biggest and most meaningful changes that occurred in me since I became a Rotarian.

This invocation by Bill Carter came at a time when I needed a wake-up call in my life, too. When I realized that the prizes from life's rat race, such as money, fame, or power, would not help me find any long-lasting meaning in life, I decided to read a few books on Mother Teresa. By reading about this true saint, I thought I could better understand her life, and also reflect some of her wisdom and good deeds in my own life. When I was half-way through a biography on her, which I carried with me to New Orleans, I had a most bizarre experience of meeting her in New Orleans.

I met Mother Teresa (or her life-size statue, to be more precise) twice in New Orleans. The first time was in December of 2007 when our family made a trip to New Orleans. During that trip, I wanted to show our daughters two things: the unimaginably huge impact Hurricane Katrina left behind in New Orleans and also the equally remarkable resilience and spirit of the citizens of New Orleans to reconstruct their temporarily broken city. Basically, I wanted our two children to feel the sheer power of Mother Nature and also see the endeavors made by human beings to overcome that formidable power. During our trip, to my surprise, we bumped into Mother Teresa's statue at an old cemetery, named Saint Louis Cemetery, which lies to the north of downtown New Orleans. I had a most surreal experience when I saw it because I happened to carry her biography with me during that entire trip. Under her statue, the following scripture was engraved:

If you pray, you will have faith
And if you have faith, you will love
And if you love, you will serve
And if you serve, you will have peace

It was then that I decided to put together all my writings about Rotary and its impact on me. I always knew that Rotary meant service, but until I read Mother Teresa's biography, I never knew that service and love are two sides of one coin. According to her, unless our service is rooted in, and starts from, faith in and love for humanity, it is not true service. Unless we feel pain while we develop that love, just like an oyster painfully grows a pearl in its soft flesh, then it is not true love. In other words, if we love someone, then we should love that person to the extent our heart actually aches. Otherwise, we are not truly in love with that person, and we cannot possibly provide true service. I don't remember the last time when I loved any person or any object to that extent. The statement under the statue of Mother Teresa definitely humbled and made a long-lasting impression on me.

Apparently Mother Teresa never had a family of her own, but more than fifty thousand needy people in India, and millions of other people around the world, regarded her as their mother because they all witnessed the "service above self" spirit in her throughout her entire life.

The second time I met Mother Teresa's statue was when I visited New Orleans again in May 2011 to participate in the Rotary International convention. There, by chance, I bumped into a group of Korean Rotarians from Busan, South Korea, who gave me an ambassadorial scholarship some twenty years ago. They wanted me to join them in the bus they rented, and together, we briefly visited the same cemetery where I met Mother Teresa's statue again. This time I thought that the smile on her face signified love and her praying hands signified service for humanity.

Both times I visited the statue of Mother Teresa, I prayed with her. I felt as if she was whispering to me: "Hello, Wooj. I know you are a Rotarian. I know you are in the business of service above self. Then, please remember this: Do Good Anyway!"

I visited the statue of Mother Teresa in New Orleans twice –
once with my family members and another time with a group of
Rotarians who gave me a Rotary International Ambassadorial
Scholarship some 20 years ago. Each time I visited her, I realized
how important it is for us Rotarians to find the cause of our service in love. From these trips I also came back with a deep sense
of responsibility toward many underprivileged people around the
world.

Epilogue

I've looked at life from both sides now
From up and down and still somehow
It's life's illusions I recall
I really don't know life at all
                    —Joni Mitchell, "Both Sides Now"

This memoir was not meant to be an autobiography because, in my definition, "autobiographies" are usually written by great people based on their heroic episodes, and I know for sure that I don't have those heroic stories under my belt. Nor do I regard myself as a great person anyway. This memoir is a collection of memorable anecdotes from the most recent chapters of my life. Many of the most important events in my life happened after I had the interview in 1989 to receive the Rotary International Ambassadorial Scholarship in Busan, Korea, to come to study in the United States.

Throughout this memoir, I tried to use humor as frequently as possible, but humor is not the theme of this book. If there is any theme or a common thread in this book, it is rather "service above self," which happens to be the slogan of Rotary International.

When I was chosen as one of the ambassadorial scholarship

recipients, Dr. K.H. Yoon, the director of Busan Rotary district, said to me, "Mr. Byun, this scholarship will turn you into a global citizen. We all wish you good luck and great success in your future. We also hope you don't forget about Rotary." Dr. Yoon was right. I think the Rotary International Ambassadorial Scholarship was one of the best events that happened to me, and the decision to join Rotary (which I did about five years after I received the scholarship) was one of the wisest decisions I ever made.

After living for more than two decades in Minnesota, one of the coldest places in the United States, I almost became a Viking myself. Sometimes I see a Norwegian face when I look at myself in the mirror. And I get tempted to raise my hand when there is a question: "Is there a Scandinavian in this room?" I hope this memoir gave the readers a glimpse of why I would raise my hand at such a moment.

Years ago, I told my godparents, Bill and Lois Clynes, that I would write a book based on the Minnesota chapter of my life. Two decades ago, I also promised many folks at the University of Minnesota Law School that I would eventually write a book based on my experience in the United States. I am glad that I kept that promise by writing this memoir, although I admit it took a much longer time than I expected.

Many good friends read or offered to read my manuscript. I would like to thank all of them. Sometimes just talking with them gave me the courage to continue to write this memoir. Some of those friends are Julie Ward, Ken Anderson, Mary Hustad, Sandy Schley, Milt Adams, Paul Mooty, Thom Winninger, Tim Murphy, Anne Labovitz, David Wagner, and the Clynes, to name just a few.

My parents and siblings in Korea, my wife Jennifer, and our two daughters (Nina and Maria) have been the cornerstones of my life while I wrote this memoir, and I would like to thank them for understanding and loving me all the years. David Halperin, my former boss in Hong Kong, who turned me into a useful man, still remains a mentor for me, and I thank him dearly. Many of my fellow Rotarians at the Rotary Club of Edina and other cities (who are too numerous to mention here, but who are mentioned throughout the book) helped me with this memoir in one way or another, and I want to express my genuine appreciation and indebtedness to them.

My friends in Korea (who are also too many to list here) always encouraged me to be me, and I would like to thank them for being there when I needed them. Were it not for my friends from my life's Hong Kong chapter (including Milbert Shin, Keith Lutz, Jon Molot, J.D. Lee, Thae Khwarg, Tom Jones, Bill Mondale, Tim O'Brien, and Sung Kim), I don't think I would have become a global citizen, so I would like to thank them, as well. (Incidentally, Sung Kim just became the new US ambassador to Korea. I wish him best of luck with his new job!)

Finally, I would like to dedicate this memoir to all the Rotarians across the globe, whom I have met, associated with, read about, spoke to, benefited from, and emulated. They gave me a scholarship, hope, inspiration, joy, friendship, and encouragement. If I make any difference in this world with my life, it is all because of their investment and trust in me. This memoir is a small token of my gratitude for their generosity. From the bottom of my heart, I sincerely thank all the Rotarians around the world.

During the past fifty years of my life, I've had many life-changing experiences, but joining the Rotary Club and learning the true meaning of "service above self" from other fellow Rotarians was certainly one of the most enriching experiences of my life. In fact, each time I associated myself with a Rotarian, that encounter or association always taught me another lesson about service. As a beneficiary of the Rotary Ambassadorial Scholarship, I always felt that I was indebted to Rotary. As I near the final pages of this memoir, I hope that this small memoir will serve as an encouragement for people, including all the scholarship recipients around the world, both past, present, and future, to join in Rotary International's endeavors to make the world a better and more peaceful place by adopting the spirit of service above self.

While writing this memoir, I had a rare opportunity to visit and reconnect with my own life. Life after joining Rotary has been truly a blessed chapter in my life, because every time I tried to pay back to Rotary, Rotary gave me more. I would like to thank all the Rotarians in Minnesota and Korea, who gladly shared their wisdom with me throughout this most exciting and enriching part of my life.

Of all the definitions of "love," I like most the following quote from Antoine de Saint-Exupery, author of *The Little Prince*, who once said, "Perhaps love is the process of my leading you gently back to yourself." If the readers can regard this memoir as an attempt by a recipient of the Rotary International Scholarship, whose life was changed dramatically by the donors of the scholarship, to return the benefit back to the Rotarians, the honor will be solely mine. People around me reminded me who I am by pouring their love on me; by writing this memoir, I wanted to show them how blessed I have been by their love.

Recently I heard from someone that the founder of Marriott Hotels once said to his employees that "service is the rent we pay for living in this world." For some people, service is a privilege; for some, it is an obligation or duty; for some, it is a luxury; and for some people, such as Rotarians, service is just a way of life. Rotarians gladly choose to be of service to others in need. I feel blessed to have met and embraced Rotary in my life.

About the Author

Woodrow "Wooj" Byun is a Minnesota-based attorney, community leader, and Rotarian. He studied linguistics and law at Seoul National University. He also obtained a master's degree in international law from Korea University, a diploma in Chinese law from Macau East West University, and a juris doctor degree from the University of Minnesota Law School. He has practiced law in Minnesota since 1994.

Wooj was born in Korea, and he has lived and worked in Seoul, Hong Kong, and Minneapolis. He served as advisor to the president of South Korea on reunification and the president of the University of Minnesota on Asian issues. Since 2012, he has been an advisory board member of the Weisman Art Museum in Minnesota.

His law practice includes a variety of corporate and personal clients. Corporate clients he served include ImageTrend, Leonard Parker Associated Architects, RSP, LG Mart, New Life Fitness, Korea Exchange Bank, ICG, and Tokyo Express, to name a few.

Wooj received a Rotary International Ambassadorial Scholarship in 1990, which was instrumental in his ability to realize his dream of becoming a global citizen. He joined Edina Rotary Club, mainly to pay back the scholarship he received from Rotary

International. He served as president of Edina Rotary Club from 2011 to 2012. He is a multiple Paul Harris Fellow. Wooj lives in Minnesota with his wife, Jennifer Park, who also became a Paul Harris Fellow, and their two daughters. He has been a dynamic speaker on the subject of "service above self." To contact him, please send him a message at his Facebook account (Woodrow Wooj Byun) or an email at woojbyun@gmail.com or visit his website: www.woodrowlaw.com.

Praise for *My Rotary Journey*

A past Rotary Ambassadorial Scholar and past president of the Rotary Club of Edina, Wooj Byun has filled his book, *My Rotary Journey*, with the kind of warmth and humor that he brings to life every day. He is proud of his Korean heritage, his family, and his affiliation with Rotary International, and he shares this pride in a delightful way. An easy read, Wooj's stories will make you laugh . . . make you cry . . . and help you understand the joy and commitment to Rotary and the "service above self" that has become the life of Wooj Byun.

—Sandra Schley, Rotary International District 5950 Governor (2009–2010)

Take a look at yourself, and America, through the eyes of Woodrow "Wooj" Byun's wry, witty, and charming memoir, and you may never see yourself, or America, in quite the same way again. Wooj, born to a Korean elementary school teacher and homemaker, but who "may be a Scandinavian" (you'll have to read the book), came to Minnesota to go to law school in his late twenties, and neither he nor Minnesota have been the same since. He learned much about America. Sample bits of wisdom: "Americans didn't fart" and "microwave oven is a must have in the American kitchen." We gained a lawyer, writer, family man, and all around compassionate human being. If you doubt, read his funny and touching account of helping 120 Korean grandparents pass the US citizenship interview. You'll have to read the book.

—Paul Zerby, former assistant attorney general of Minnesota; former Minneapolis city councilman; author of *The Grass*.

Hearing Wooj's Rotary story touched me; reading the details inspired me. As a Rotarian myself who is committed to the mission and activities of Rotary, I find Wooj's story most compelling and interesting. His memoir brings Rotary to life, reinforces its impact, and makes it all so real. The memoir carries not only great stories, but it also conveys important messages, too.

—Irene Kelly, Rotary International District 5950 assistant governor (2011–2012)

Wooj shares his tales of living in Minnesota in an entertaining and heartfelt manner. His stories offer a window into his formative years in Korea and illustrate how the values his parents imparted to him shaped his life as a Rotarian in the US. Wooj's heartwarming stories paint a picture of someone who truly lives his life within the Rotary's motto of "service above self." His loyalty and integrity are a constant thread throughout the book. He maintains a positive attitude and a can-do spirit, even when faced with seemingly insurmountable obstacles. After reading the story of this "My Rotary Journey," it is clear that Wooj has touched—and changed—countless lives over the years, starting with his own as a Rotary Ambassadorial Scholar.

—Diann Kirby, International District 5950 governor (2013–2014)

This book is a compelling story of giving and receiving, helping people find their ways, and being a friend to all peoples! Wooj and his story are both gift to making the world a better place. Read it, reflect on it, and be inspired by it!

—Thomas J. Winninger, CSMA; bestselling author of six books

The humorous and heart-warming stories in *My Rotary Journey* blend the better of two cultures to form the life experiences of Woodrow "Wooj" Byun. A scholar with a servant heart, Wooj tells the tale of immigrating to the United States from South Korea, bringing with him a reverence for elders and tradition instilled by his father and a hilarious irreverence for being the only non-Caucasian in a Minnesota meeting room. With the help of a scholarship extended by Rotary International, Wooj has managed to create his own personal success story only to attempt at every turn to repay those who've helped him along the way. Funny. Poignant. A real-life example of servant leadership. *My Rotary Journey* is terrific!

–Angela Johnson, Editor of Edina Magazine